Be Your Type of Super
The Journey From Freshman To Graduate

By Dena Wiggins, MBA, CPC

ISBN-13: 978-0-578-55699-4

Dedicated To The Next Generation

Of Possibility! Your Type of Super

Is Amazing, Needed & Yours To

Explore, Discover & Be.

Table of Contents

BE

Verb

1. Exist
2. Occur, Take Place

YOUR

Determiner

Belonging To Or Associated With The Person Or People The Speaker Is Addressing

TYPE OF

Noun

a person or thing symbolizing or exemplifying the ideal or defining characteristics of something

SUPER

Combining Form Prefix

1. Above, Over, Beyond
2. To A Great Degree

Be

Isn't About Doing A
Bunch of Stuff But Being
YOU

Your

This Is About You
Discovering Your Answers

Type Of

This Is About You Understanding
Your Uniqueness

Super

That Will Help You Unlock What
Comes After The Prefix Super

What Do You Value?

When you start a new thing, you bring your knowledge, personality, insight and values to it. Values are your Principles or standards of behavior, your judgement of what's important in life.

Everywhere you go and in everything you do, you have the opportunity to bring what your values to it. It's like your signature. Before you begin the exercises, take a moment and check into your values that YOU bring to the experience and hold yourself accountable to maintain those values throughout the exercises.

Pick the most important three values from the treasure chest of values below. If you do not see your top three below, add them!

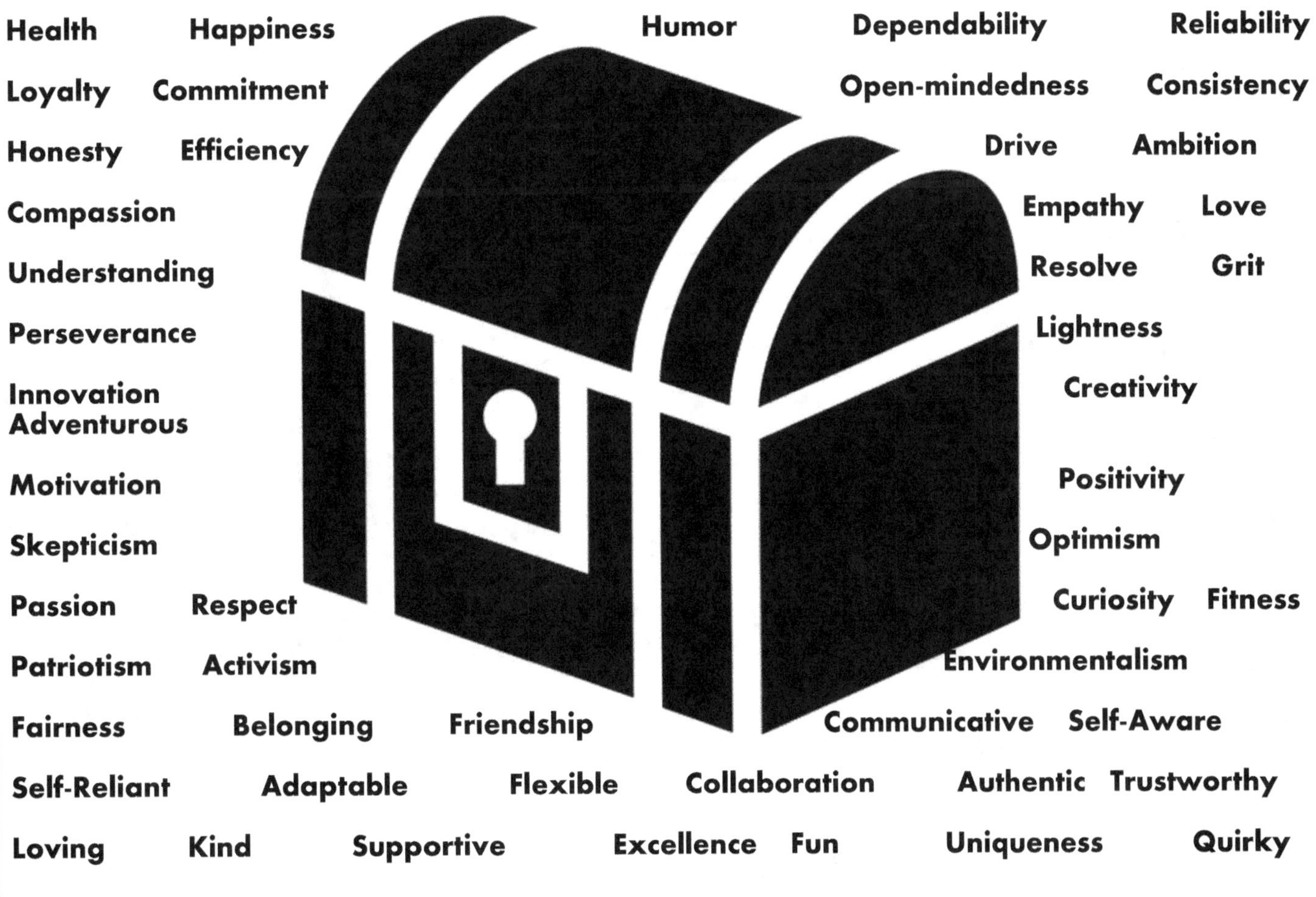

These exercises are designed for you to unlock your type of super and letting this insight inform your decisions and actions!

It requires you to bring an open mind, honesty, being ok with not having all of the answers, sticking with it through the end, open to believing your life has meaning just because YOU exist, open to believing you have a super that gives your life MORE meaning.

And I will bring my values of:

1. ______________________

2. ______________________ and

3. ______________________

to the Be Your Type of Super exercises and intentionally (on purpose) throughout my life.

____

Sign Here. This your commitment to yourself and to your emerging type of super

KNOWING

"Knowing yourself is the beginning of all wisdom."

Aristotle

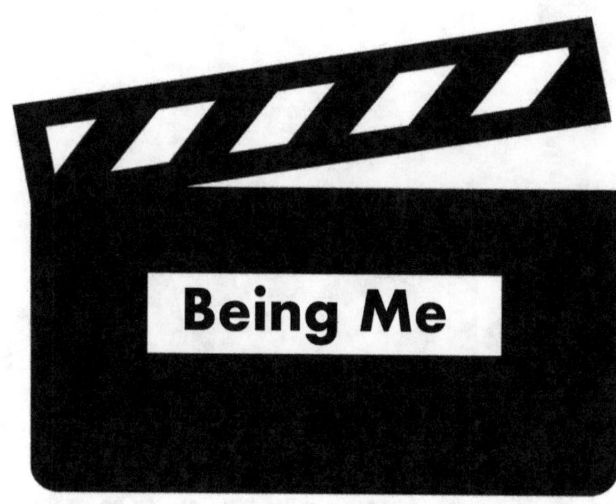

If you were to watch a movie of your life titled, Being Me, describe what you see, in detail, knowing the characters & scenes like you do.

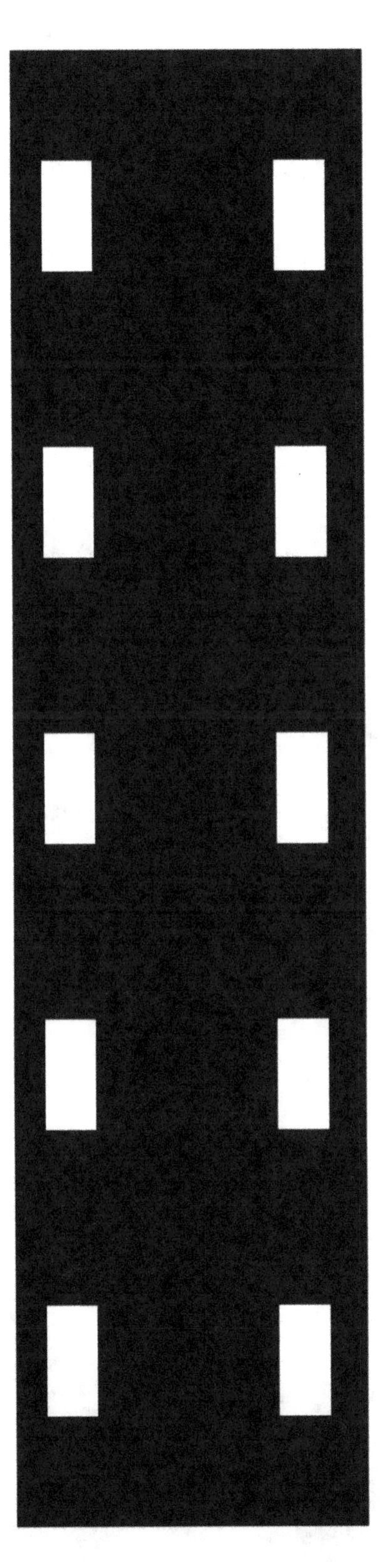

Think of one of your favorite movies. In the beginning of the movie, you see the main character being "normal" in his or her "ordinary world."

As the story progresses, you see the plot thicken or the type of journey he or she is on and the different things he or she will overcome to triumph over a major problem.

This is called the Hero's or Heroine's Journey. The steps throughout the journey reveal the Hero's or Heroine's type of super.

"It's common to think that stuff only happens in the movies or to give hope to a different possibility, like when the underdog rises. But what if the *real* reason we love some movies is because they are relatable? What if the hero's and heroine's journey happen all the time without the lights and cameras?"

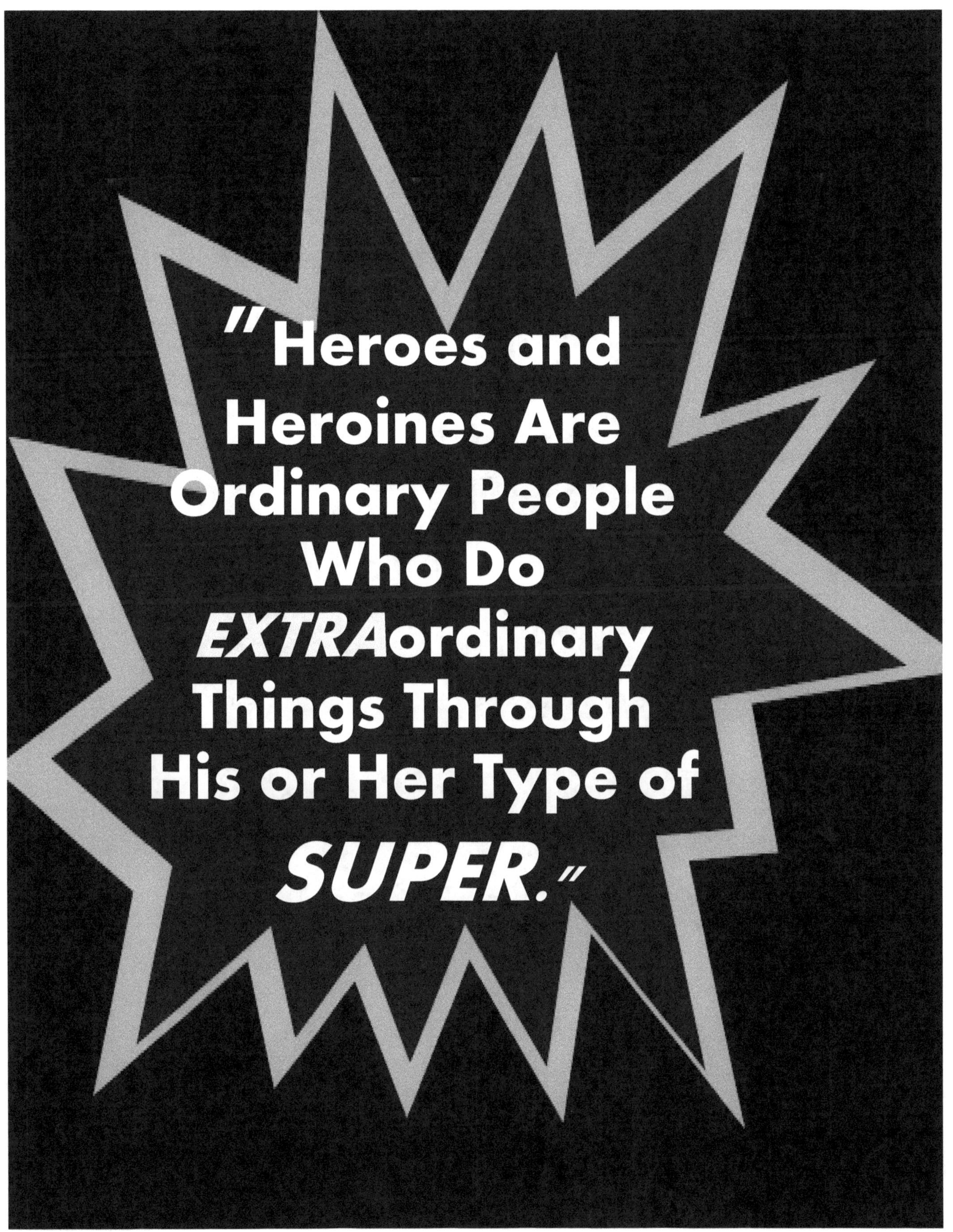
"Heroes and
Heroines Are
Ordinary People
Who Do
EXTRAordinary
Things Through
His or Her Type of
SUPER."

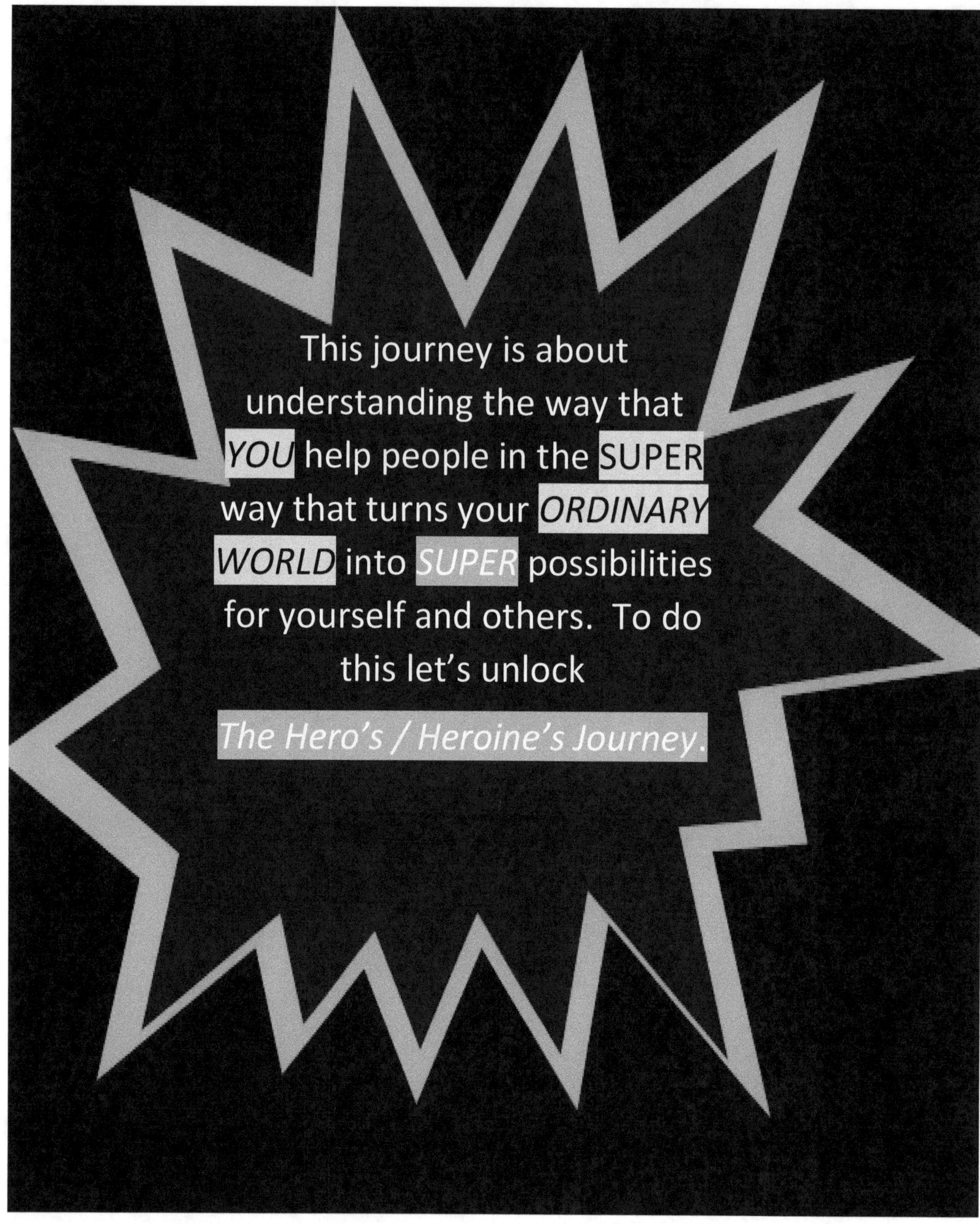
This journey is about understanding the way that YOU help people in the SUPER way that turns your ORDINARY WORLD into SUPER possibilities for yourself and others. To do this let's unlock
The Hero's / Heroine's Journey.

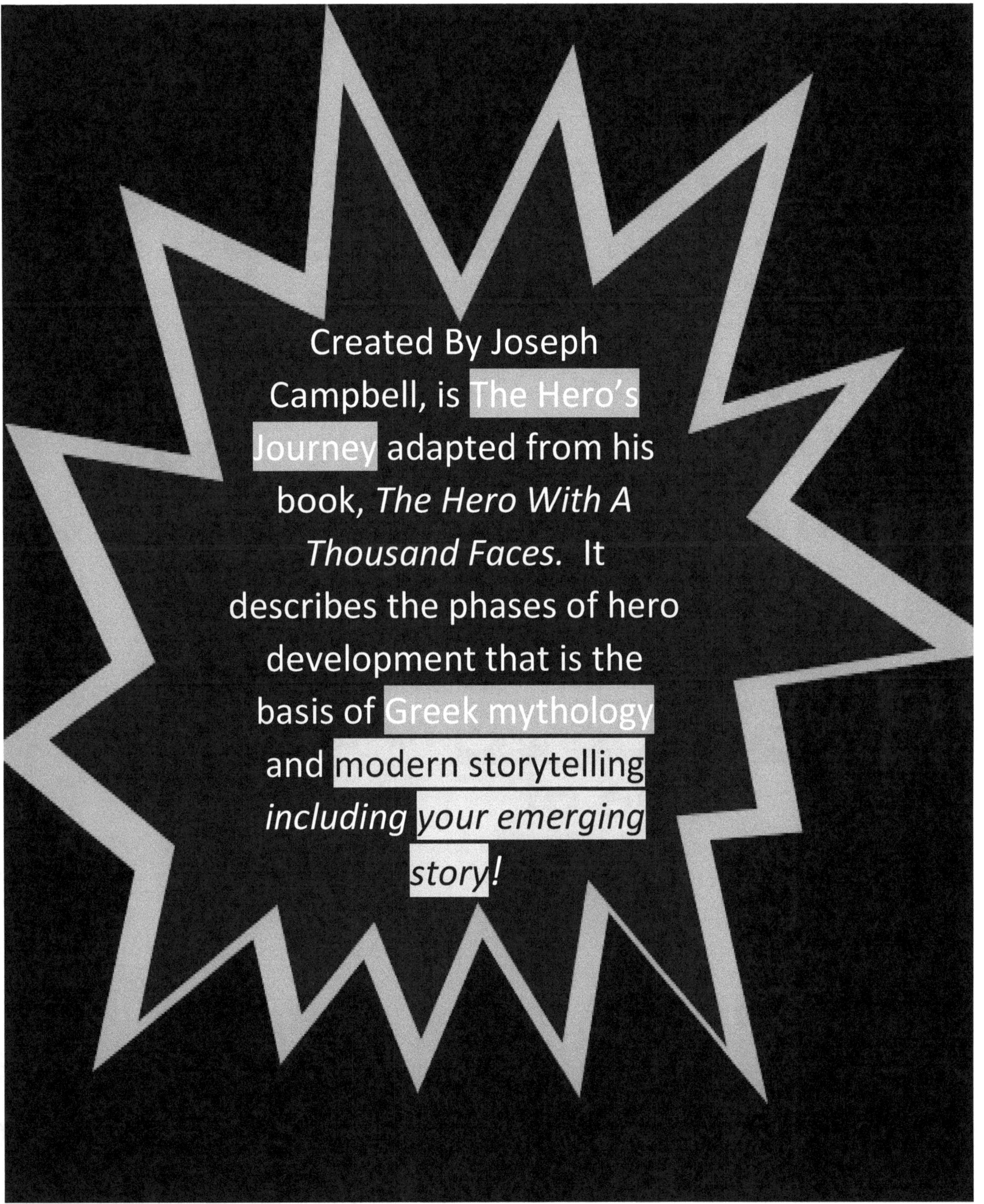
Created By Joseph Campbell, is The Hero's Journey adapted from his book, *The Hero With A Thousand Faces.* It describes the phases of hero development that is the basis of Greek mythology and modern storytelling *including your emerging story!*

"If you completed the Be Your Type of Super Rising Purpose Peep Workbook, you will find additional steps to the Hero's & Heroine's Journey. The additional steps will connect to ways for you to BE your type of *SUPER*."

The Hero's Or Heroine's Journey Unlocked

The hero or heroine is living in the ordinary world. The ordinary world is the day-to-day routine or norm of the hero or heroine	 **The Ordinary World** 
 **The Call To Adventure** 	This is the event that begins the journey. This event shakes up the normal, ordinary routine. Sometimes the change is welcomed by the hero or heroine. Most of the time, the call comes as an unexpected challenge or problem.
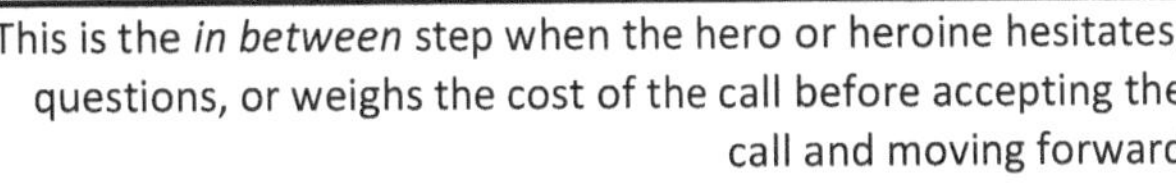 This is the *in between* step when the hero or heroine hesitates, questions, or weighs the cost of the call before accepting the call and moving forward	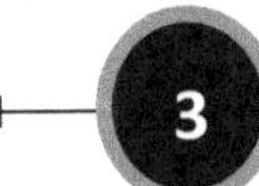 **The Refusal of the Call** 
  **Meets The Mentor**	The hero or heroine meets with a mentor who guides them. The mentor provides wisdom for the steps ahead. The age of the mentor does not matter.
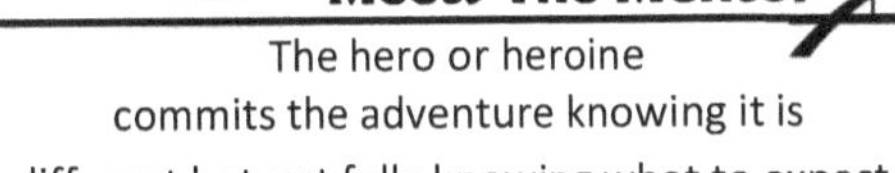 The hero or heroine commits the adventure knowing it is different but not fully knowing what to expect.	 **Crossing The First Threshold**
 **Tests, Allies &Enemies** 	Allies show up and partner with the hero or heroine. The protagonist is also revealed.
The hero of heroine comes to the center of the journey and is met with tests that reveal the treasure of the story.	 **Approach To The Innermost Cave** 
 **The Ordeal** 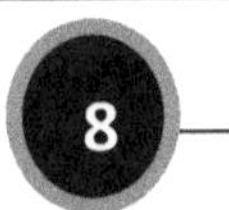	The hero or heroine is pushed to give up completely. This is when the person who began the journey transforms to the hero or heroine. Before this happens, the hero or heroine feels they must give up.
The hero or heroine receives a reward for conquering the ordeal.	 **The Reward** 
 **The Road Back** 	The hero or heroine returns to the ordinary world transformed.
The hero or heroine is reborn as a person with the knowledge of his or her *extra*ordinary type of super.	 **The Resurrection** 
 **Return To Share The Reward** 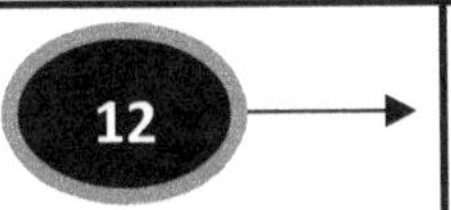	The hero or heroine returns to the ordinary world with the elixir to share with the ordinary world and as demonstration of his or her type of super.
The hero or heroine realizes the journey is continuous and each version of it begins with the call to adventure.	 **Realization**  

What Are Your Thoughts?

The Hero's Or Heroine's Journey
Percy Jackson

Percy is thought to have ADHD and dyslexia and is unaware that he is a demigod.	1 The Ordinary World
2 The Call To Adventure	On a school trip, his "teacher" attacks him and he responds with superhuman powers after his mother disappears.
When Percy learns the special camp, he is sent to is for demigods, he does not believe he belongs.	3 The Refusal of the Call
4 Meets The Mentor	Mr. Brunner is revealed to be Chiron, a gifted mentor who guides and trains Percy along the way.
Poseidon acknowledges Percy as his son and assigns him the task to retrieve Zeus' lightning rod.	5 Crossing The First Threshold
6 Tests, Allies & Enemies	Percy takes Annabeth, daughter of Athena and Grover with him on the journey to retrieve the lightning rod. They battle against Medusa and gain the friendship of Luke Castellan.
Percy and friends enter the realm of Hades and approach the Chimera who guards Hades.	7 Approach To The Innermost Cave
8 The Ordeal	Hades accuses Percy of stealing the Helm of Darkness and threatens him. Percy and friends escape.
Percy learns that Ares was the mastermind behind the stolen items.	9 The Reward
10 The Road Back	Percy challenges Ares and wins back the stolen items
Percy is reconnected with his mother, who was kidnapped by Hades.	11 Resurrection
12 Return To Share The Reward	Percy returns the lightening rod to Zeus who allows him to return to the camp.
Luke turns on Percy and it is revealed Luke was the thief as a plot to overthrow the gods. Percy is injured and is given the choice to stay at the camp or return home with his mother. Percy decides to return home with his mother.	13 Realization

What Do You See?

The Hero's Or Heroine's Journey Divergent

Beatrice is 16 and living in a dystopian and post-apocalyptic Chicago where people are divided into factions based on human virtues. Sixteen is the year of the aptitude test to determine which faction will be his or her permanent group.

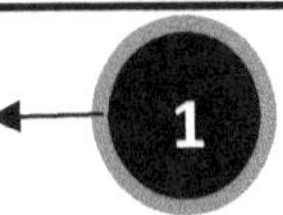

The Ordinary World

The Call To Adventure

Beatrice learns she is divergent and will never fit into and one of the factions. Being found to be divergent is dangerous to the government structure.

To remain safe, Beatrice pretends to be one faction to hide her true nature and not be taken captive by the government.

The Refusal of the Call

Meets The Mentor

Tori Wu is Beatrice's first mentor who is the first to discover she is divergent. She warns her to keep her true nature a secret. Four becomes another mentor.

Beatrice passes the initiation Into Dauntless else she be exiled and factionless.

Crossing The First Threshold

Tests, Allies & Enemies

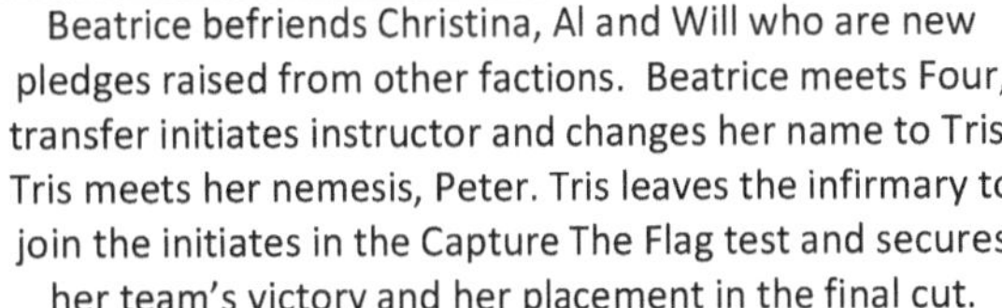

Beatrice befriends Christina, Al and Will who are new pledges raised from other factions. Beatrice meets Four, transfer initiates instructor and changes her name to Tris. Tris meets her nemesis, Peter. Tris leaves the infirmary to join the initiates in the Capture The Flag test and secures her team's victory and her placement in the final cut.

Tris visits Caleb who tells her that Erudite is planning to overthrow Abnegation and become the ruling faction.

7

Approach To The Innermost Cave

The Ordeal

Tris' Dauntless faction are injected with a serum that allows the Erudite to control their mind. Tris and other Dauntless must pretend to be mind controlled. Tris' mom is killed while saving her from execution and Four is discovered to be divergent and captured.

Tris finds Four and uses his secret to break his mind control.

The Reward

The Road Back

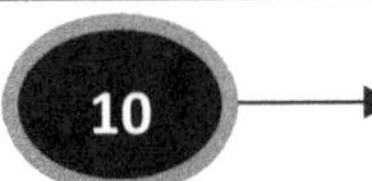

Tris and Four enter the central control room and inject Jeanine, Erudite's leader with the mind control cerum forcing her to end the mind control.

Tris uses her divergent style of creative thinking to force the Erudite leader to release the mind control program.

Resurrection

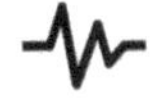

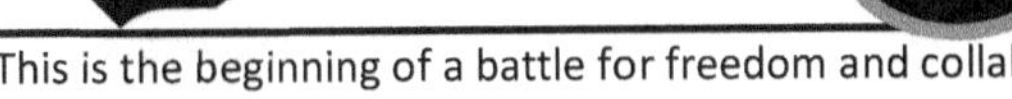

Return To Share The Reward

12

Tris and Four escape the compound and board a train out of the complex.

This is the beginning of a battle for freedom and collaboration.

Realization

What Did You See?

The Hero's Or Heroine's Journey Wonder Woman

Diana is an Amazon, daughter of Queen Hippolyta, living in Themyscira, which is man less.	1	**The Ordinary World**
The Call To Adventure	2	US Air Force Steve Trevor is shot down and crashes on the island of Hippolyta. Diana meets, fights and defeats him and takes him to the Amazons.
Diana wants to return Steve to his country but her mother insists she stay in Themyscira and guard Ares' cell. Ares escapes.	3	**The Refusal of the Call**
Meets The Mentor	4	Diana takes Steve back to his country with the double task of capturing Ares. Steve becomes a mentor guiding Diana in the customs of the new world.
The presence of Ares in the new world causes increased violence. Diana and Steve are attacked by thugs and demigod, Deimos.	5	**Crossing The First Threshold**
Tests, Allies & Enemies	6	Diana and Steve discover a gateway to the underworld guarded by members of a cult of Ares. Diana tries to attack Ares but is subdued by harpies and saved by Steve. The Amazons join the battle. Alexa provides Diana with a secret weapon. Hades removes the cuffs from Ares making mortal in battle.
Ares and his army attack Washington DC and an epic battle ensues.	7	**Approach To The Innermost Cave**
The Ordeal	8	Ares influences the President of the United States who orders as nuclear missile aimed at Themyscira. Steve shoots down the missile. Dianna overtakes Ares.
Diana has her first kiss.	9	**The Reward**
The Road Back	10	Diana returns to Themyscira but misses the outside world and Steve.
Diana accepts the role as channel between men and women from her mother.	11	**Resurrection**
Return To Share The Reward	12	Diana stays in NYC to use her powers as needed.
Diana realizes she is creating a new reality of mutual respect and acceptance.	13	**Realization**

How Did You See Things?

The Hero's Or Heroine's Journey

The Black Panther Example for High Schoolers

T'Challa is heir to the throne of futuristic Wakanda, which looks like a third world country to others. His country possesses vibranium, which is transformed into sophisticated modern technologies.	 **The Ordinary World** 
 **The Call To Adventure** 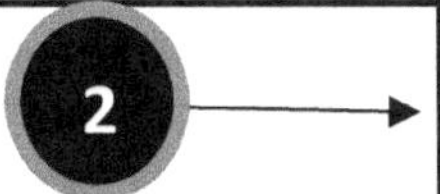	T'Challa's father, T'Chaka, is killed and T'Challa is to be crowned king of Wakanda.
T'Challa does not believe he is ready. He questions his ability to lead like his father. He awkwardly defends his crown against a challenger, M'Buku, persuading him to yield rather than die.	 **The Refusal of the Call** 
  **Meets The Mentor**	T'Challa's mentors are his father, whom he meets in the spirit realm after ingesting vibranium. His earthly mentor is his father's best friend, Zuri.
Shortly after T'Challa is crowned king, his first mission is the bring back Klaue, who stole Wakandan artifacts and threatens the secrecy and safety of the country.	 **Crossing The First Threshold**
 **Tests, Allies &Enemies** 	T'Challa's allies that help him are his sister, Shuri his past love, Nakia, Ross from the new world, the leader of his army Okoye. He also meets his cousin & fierce enemy.
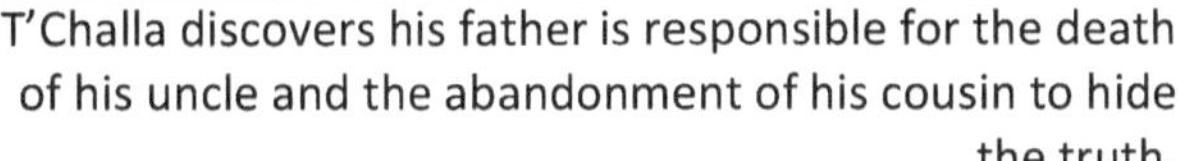 T'Challa discovers his father is responsible for the death of his uncle and the abandonment of his cousin to hide the truth.	 **Approach To The Innermost Cave** 
 **The Ordeal** 	Erik returns to Wakanda and defeats T'Challa for the throne. T'Challa is severely wounded and thought dead. T'Challa is rescued by M'Buku in retribution for his kindness. T'Challa returns with his allies to defeat Erik.
T'Challa realizes the resources of Wakanda have a higher purpose and reach.	 **The Reward** 
 **The Road Back** 	T'Challa realizes the truth that Erik came to share, there are people who can be empowered by Wakanda and knowing their heritage.
T'Challa realizes his purpose is not to lead like his father T'Chaka but to *lead like T'Challa*.	 **The Resurrection** 
 **Return To Share The Reward** 	T'Challa returns to Wakanda creating a new version of leadership through empowering others of possibility through the technological advancements of Wakanda.
This is one chapter of T'Challa's Hero's Journey. T'Challa also played a role in the Hero's & Heroine's Journey of Shuri, Okoye, Ross, T'Chaka & others.	 **Realization**  

What Would You Change?

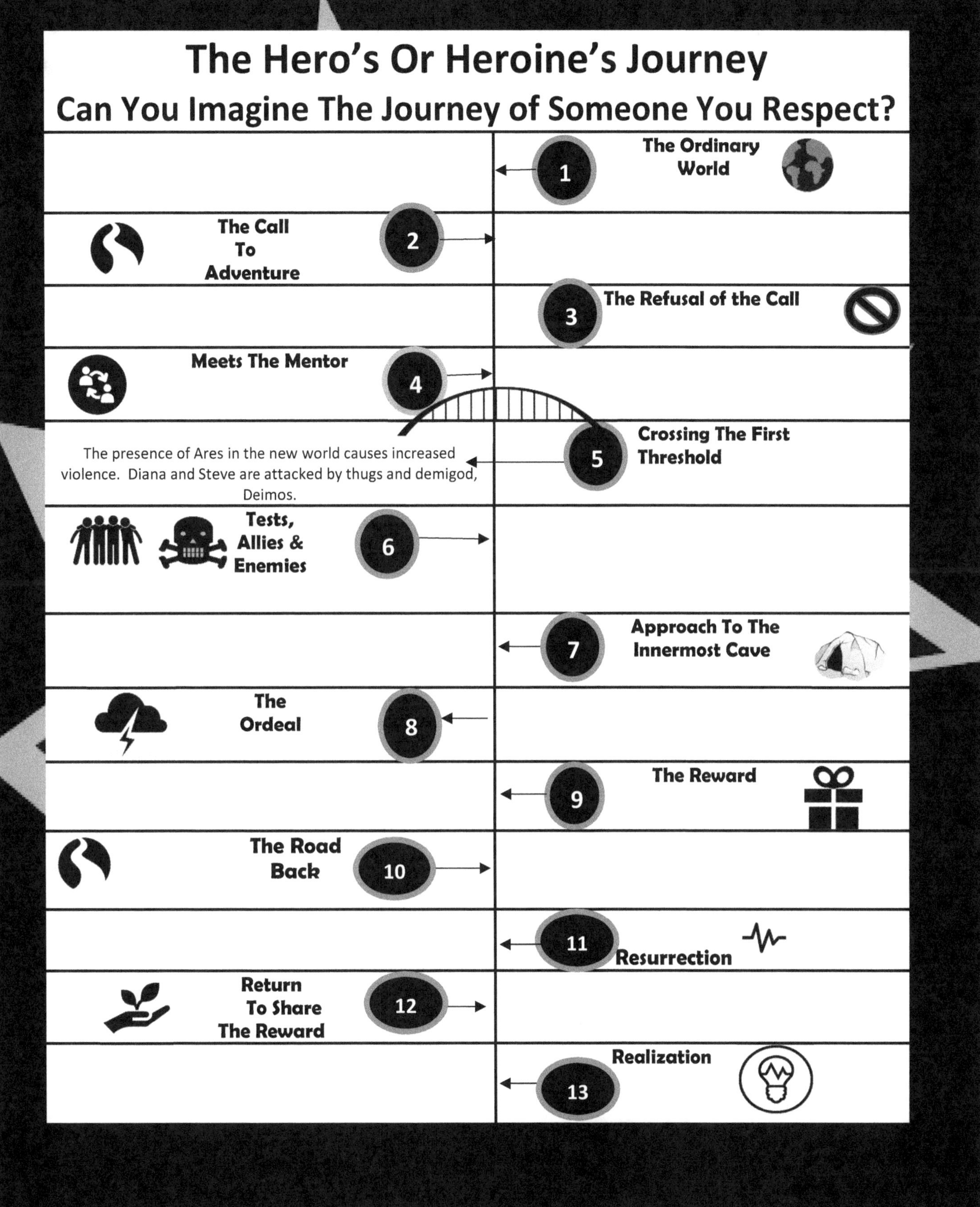
The Hero's Or Heroine's Journey
Can You Imagine The Journey of Someone You Respect?
1
The Ordinary World
The Call To Adventure
2
3
The Refusal of the Call
Meets The Mentor
4
The presence of Ares in the new world causes increased violence. Diana and Steve are attacked by thugs and demigod, Deimos.
5
Crossing The First Threshold
Tests, Allies & Enemies
6
7
Approach To The Innermost Cave
The Ordeal
8
9
The Reward
The Road Back
10
11
Resurrection
Return To Share The Reward
12
Realization
13

What Surprised You?

Do You Recognize Any Of The Characters?

Have You Been an Ally Character In Someone Else's Journey?

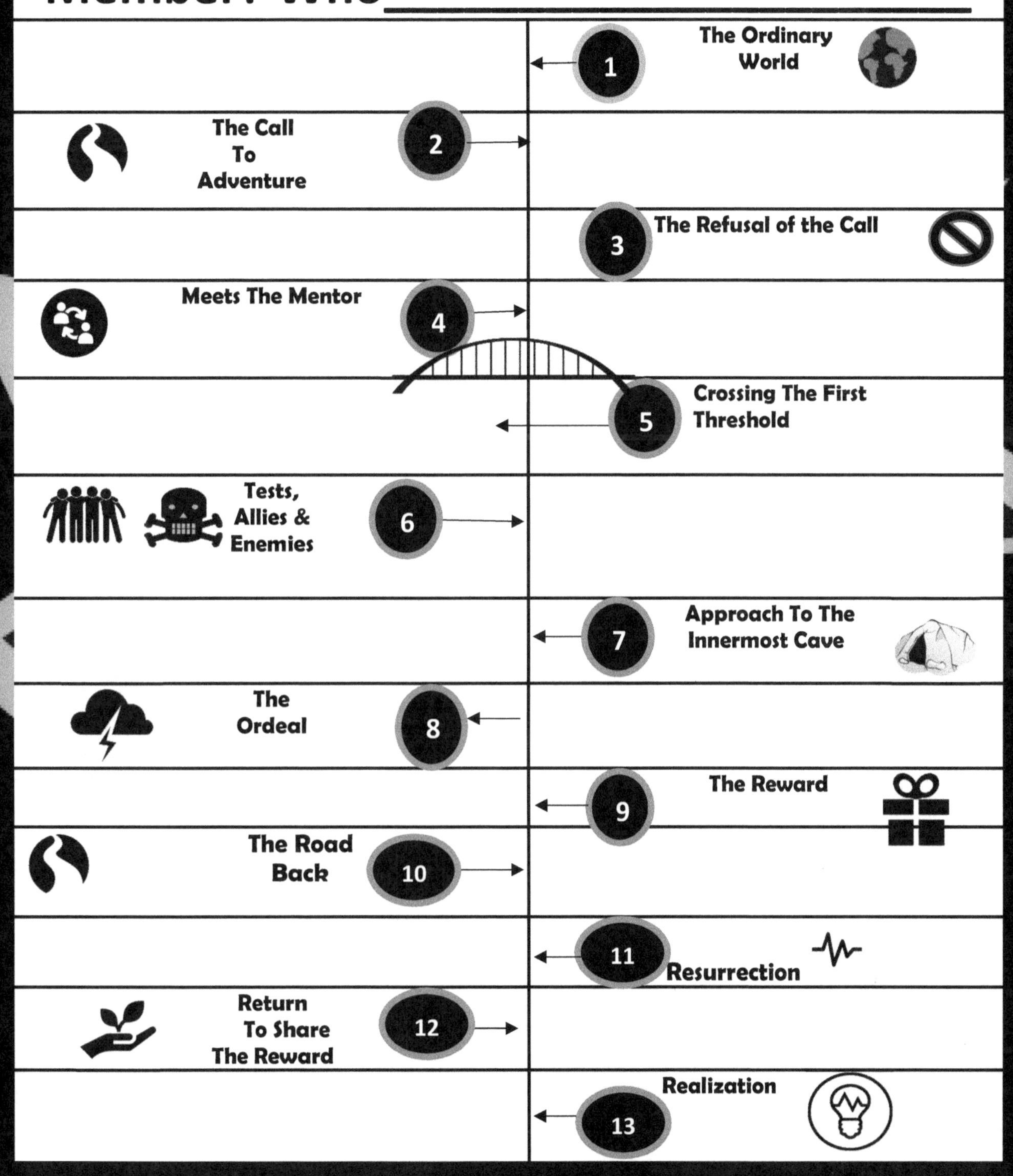
The Hero's Or Heroine's Journey
Can You Imagine The Journey of A Family Member? Who__________________________
1
The Ordinary World
The Call To Adventure
2
3
The Refusal of the Call
Meets The Mentor
4
5
Crossing The First Threshold
Tests, Allies & Enemies
6
7
Approach To The Innermost Cave
The Ordeal
8
9
The Reward
The Road Back
10
11
Resurrection
Return To Share The Reward
12
13
Realization

What Did You Learn?

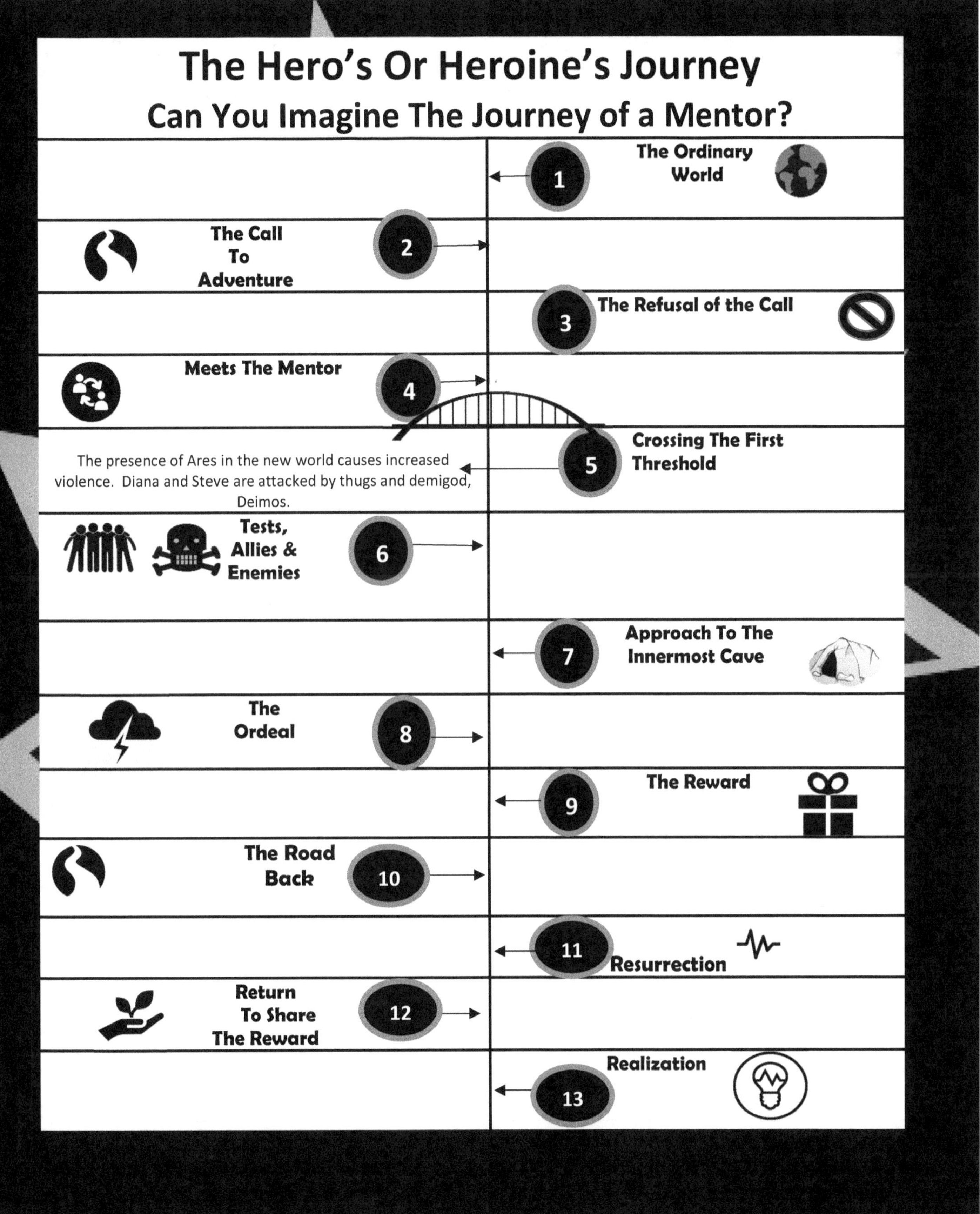

The Hero's Or Heroine's Journey
Can You Imagine The Journey of a Mentor?
1
The Ordinary World
2
The Call To Adventure
3
The Refusal of the Call
4
Meets The Mentor
5
Crossing The First Threshold
The presence of Ares in the new world causes increased violence. Diana and Steve are attacked by thugs and demigod, Deimos.
6
Tests, Allies & Enemies
7
Approach To The Innermost Cave
8
The Ordeal
9
The Reward
10
The Road Back
11
Resurrection
12
Return To Share The Reward
13
Realization

What Did You Learn?

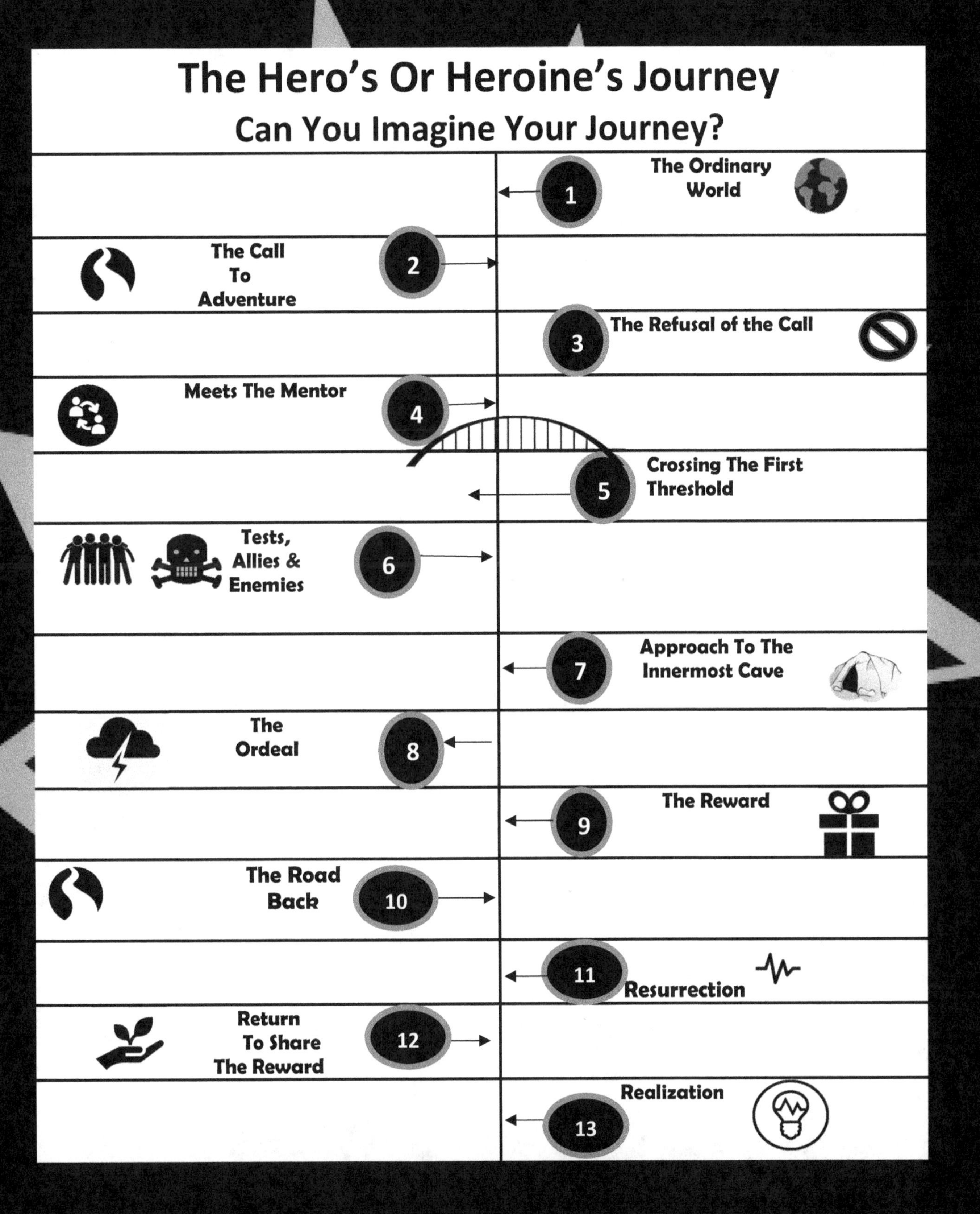
The Hero's Or Heroine's Journey
Can You Imagine Your Journey?
1 The Ordinary World
2 The Call To Adventure
3 The Refusal of the Call
4 Meets The Mentor
5 Crossing The First Threshold
6 Tests, Allies & Enemies
7 Approach To The Innermost Cave
8 The Ordeal
9 The Reward
10 The Road Back
11 Resurrection
12 Return To Share The Reward
13 Realization

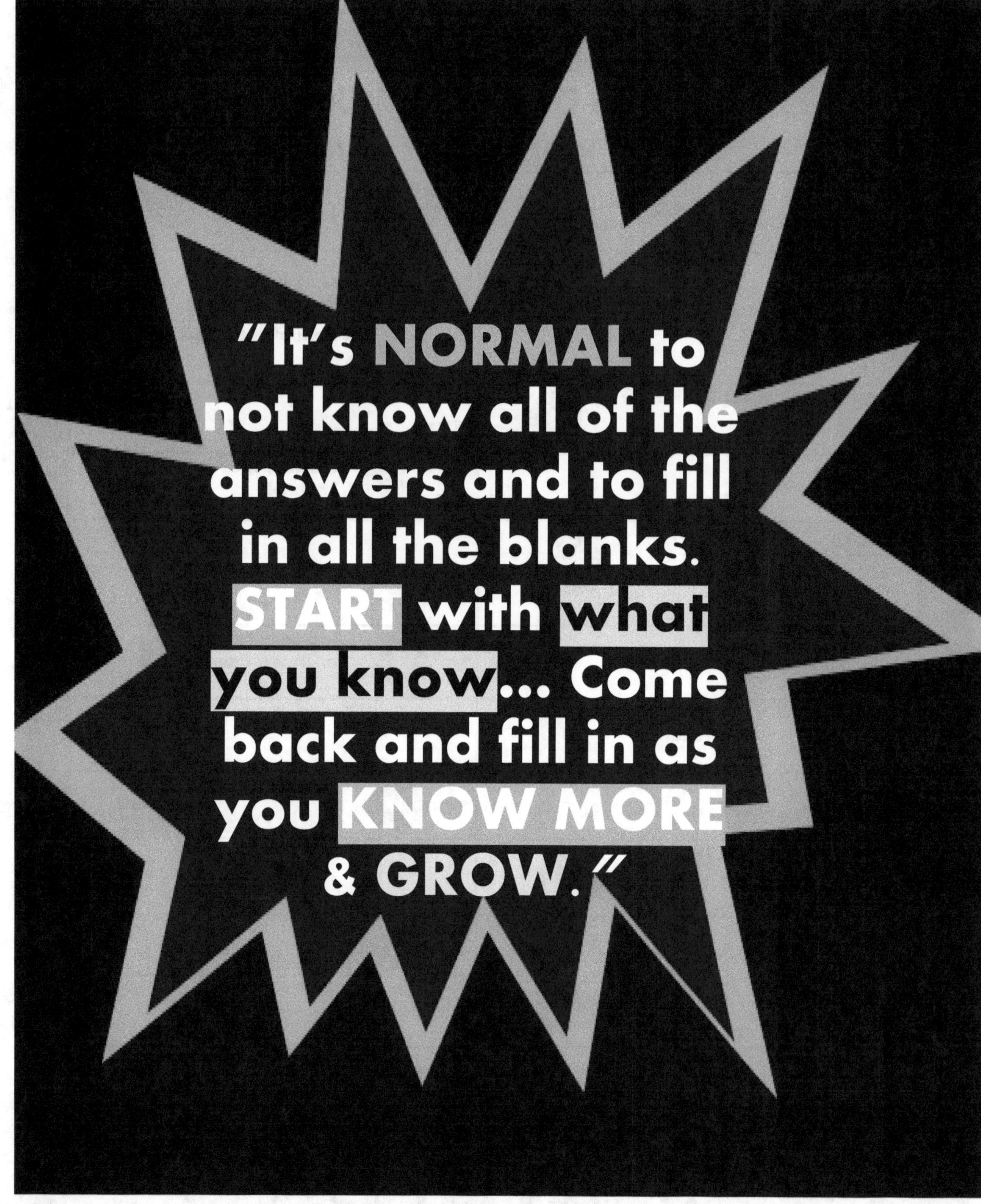
"It's NORMAL to
not know all of the
answers and to fill
in all the blanks.
START with what
you know... Come
back and fill in as
you KNOW MORE
& GROW."

What Did You Learn?

Who Are Your Mentors & What Did They Teach You?

Who Are Your Allies?

Observations About The Hero's / Heroine's Journey

HEROS/HEROINES

are everyday people who learn they are super at or about something actionable, a character trait or quality

Real Life Takes

more than 3 hours to tell a story like a movie! Some journeys take months, years or several times coming to the same step before going further

THE JOURNEY

is also called the path to purpose. It is a journey to Understand who you are and how who you are helps others

EVERYONE HAS

stuf to overcome. Everyone has ordeals, people that are **for and against** them and times they want to quit just before the BREAK through

EVERYTIME

cHAnGe happens, there is an adjustment & the question is how much and **how long** it will take to get **used to** it

WE ALL NEED

help sometimes from both friends who believe in us and show up for us & from mentors who share **wisdom** & **guide** us along the way

Just when you think you've gotten used to change, there will come a new call to adventure that begins another journey. Have you noticed that a lot of movies have sequels after it seems the story is complete?

Observations About The Hero's / Heroine's Journey

RELATIONSHIPS MATTER

- ✓ Mentors Believe You Can Do It
- ✓ Friends Journey With You & Will Help You
- ✓ Focus On Friends & What Is Good In Your Life During Times of Trouble
- ✓ People & Things That Come Against You Have A Purpose—They Push You Toward Your Super *If You Do Not Give UP!*

IMPACT

- ✓ Every Journey Starts In The Ordinary World
- ✓ Calls To Adventure Can Move You Out of The Ordinary World Also Called Comfort Zone
- ✓ You Have The Choice To Accept The Call
- ✓ Trials, Tests & Challenges May Make You Feel Like Quitting Just Before *YOUR* Super Is Revealed That Gets You To A Breakthrough

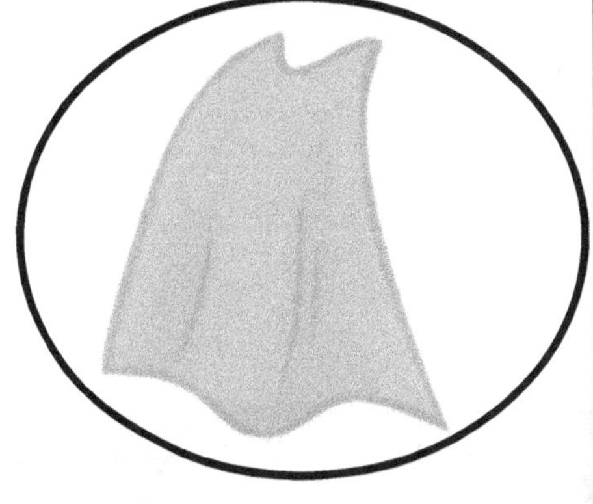

GROWTH

- ✓ You Grow Into Your Super Throughout Your Hero Or Heroine Journey
- ✓ The Things You Learn Are For You During Your Journey & To Take Back To The Ordinary World
- ✓ Being Super In The Ordinary World Requires Practice So You Don't Forget Your Super

The Hero's / Heroine's Journey Relationship Reflection

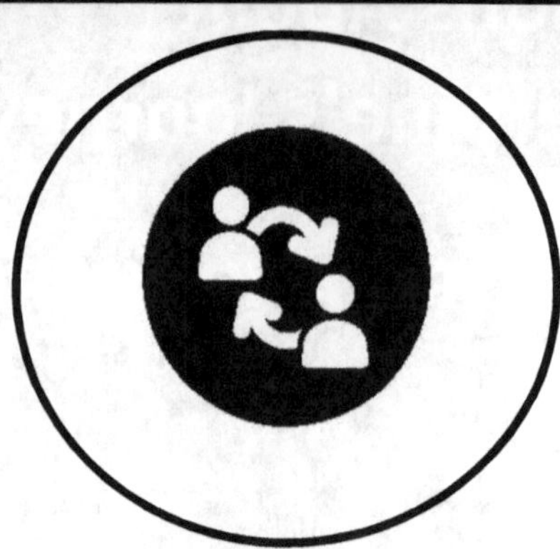

Who Are Your Mentors That Believe You Can Do It?

Who Are Your Allies That Share Your Goals & Direction?

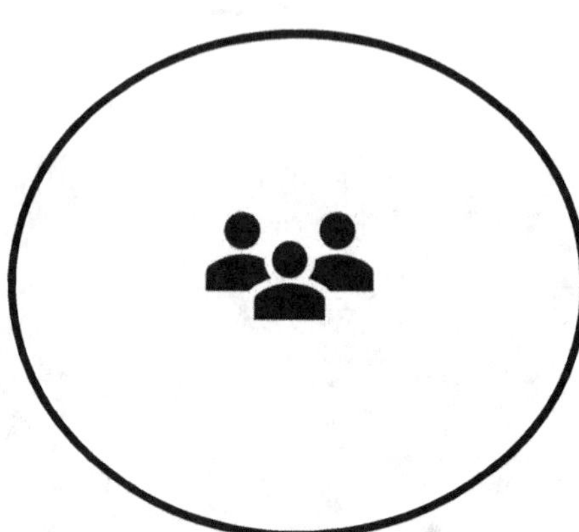

Who Are Your Friends, Your Tribe That Are There In Good Times & Bad Times?

The Hero's / Heroine's Journey Impact Reflection

What Moves You Out of Your Ordinary World (Comfort Zone)?

What Are You Really Passionate About?

Who Receives The Gifts You Take Back To The Ordinary World?

The Hero's / Heroine's Journey Growth Reflection

What Changed From The Beginning of Your Journey To Now?

What skills or knowledge are you building?

Who Supports How You Are Growing & Changing?

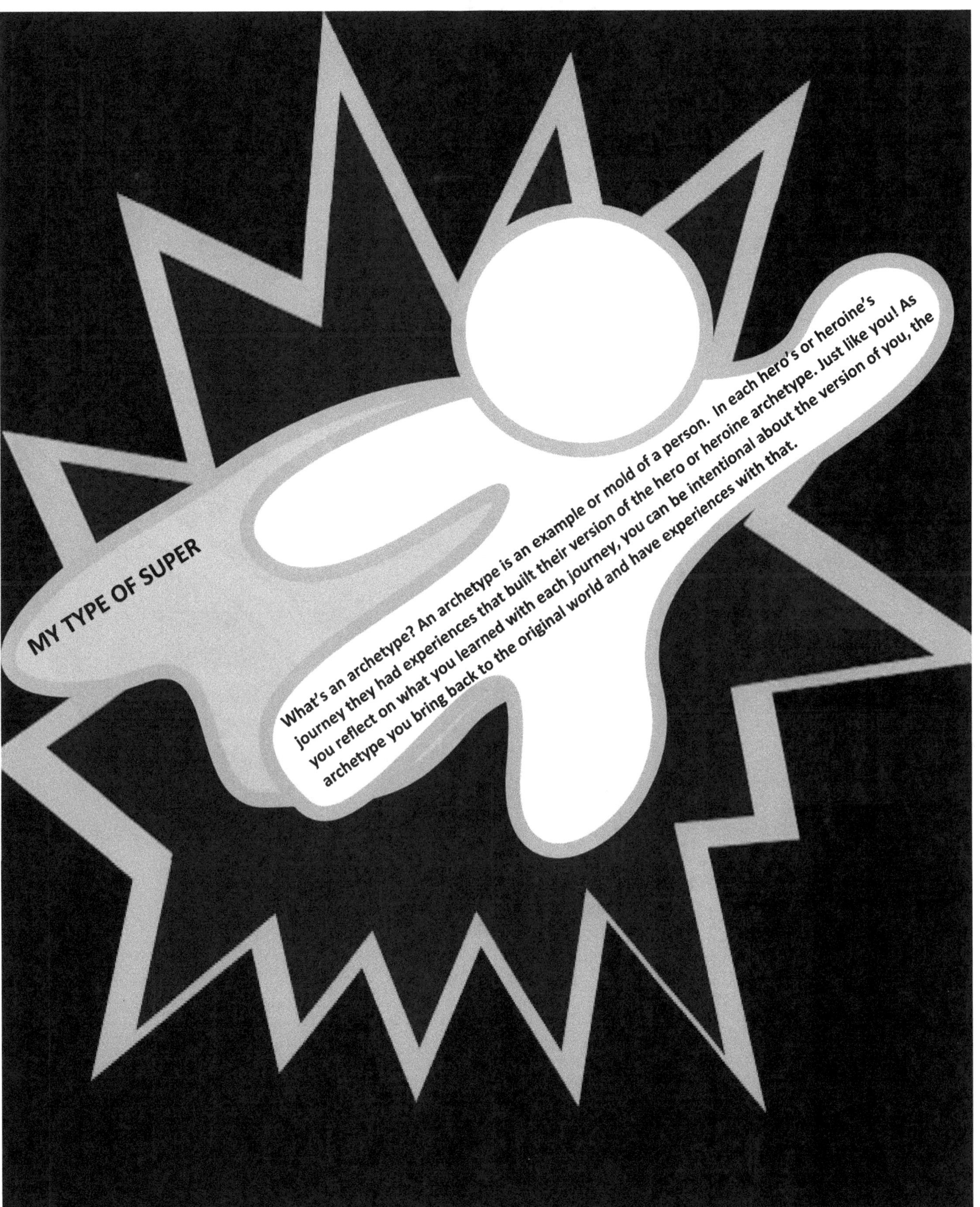
MY TYPE OF SUPER
What's an archetype? An archetype is an example or mold of a person. In each hero's or heroine's journey they had experiences that built their version of the hero or heroine archetype. Just like you! As you reflect on what you learned with each journey, you can be intentional about the version of you, the archetype you bring back to the original world and have experiences with that.

"You will experience different aspects of your type of super as you learn more about what it means and what you bring to it with your values and experiences. Now is a great time to experience purpose fluidity. Purpose fluidity happens when you find out how to serve others with your super. As you grow and change so will how you serve with and from your super."

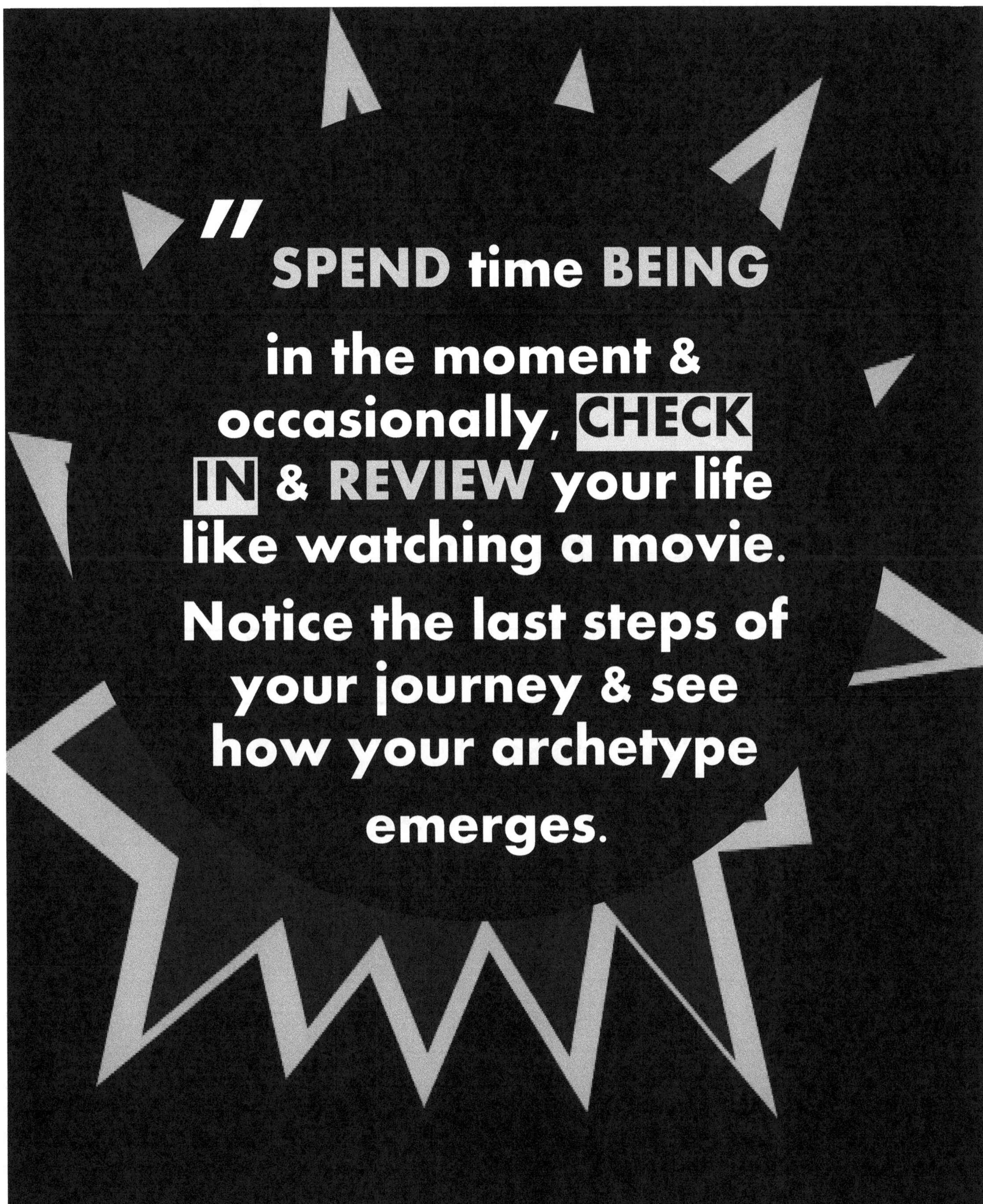
"SPEND time BEING
in the moment &
occasionally, CHECK
IN & REVIEW your life
like watching a movie.
Notice the last steps of
your journey & see
how your archetype
emerges.

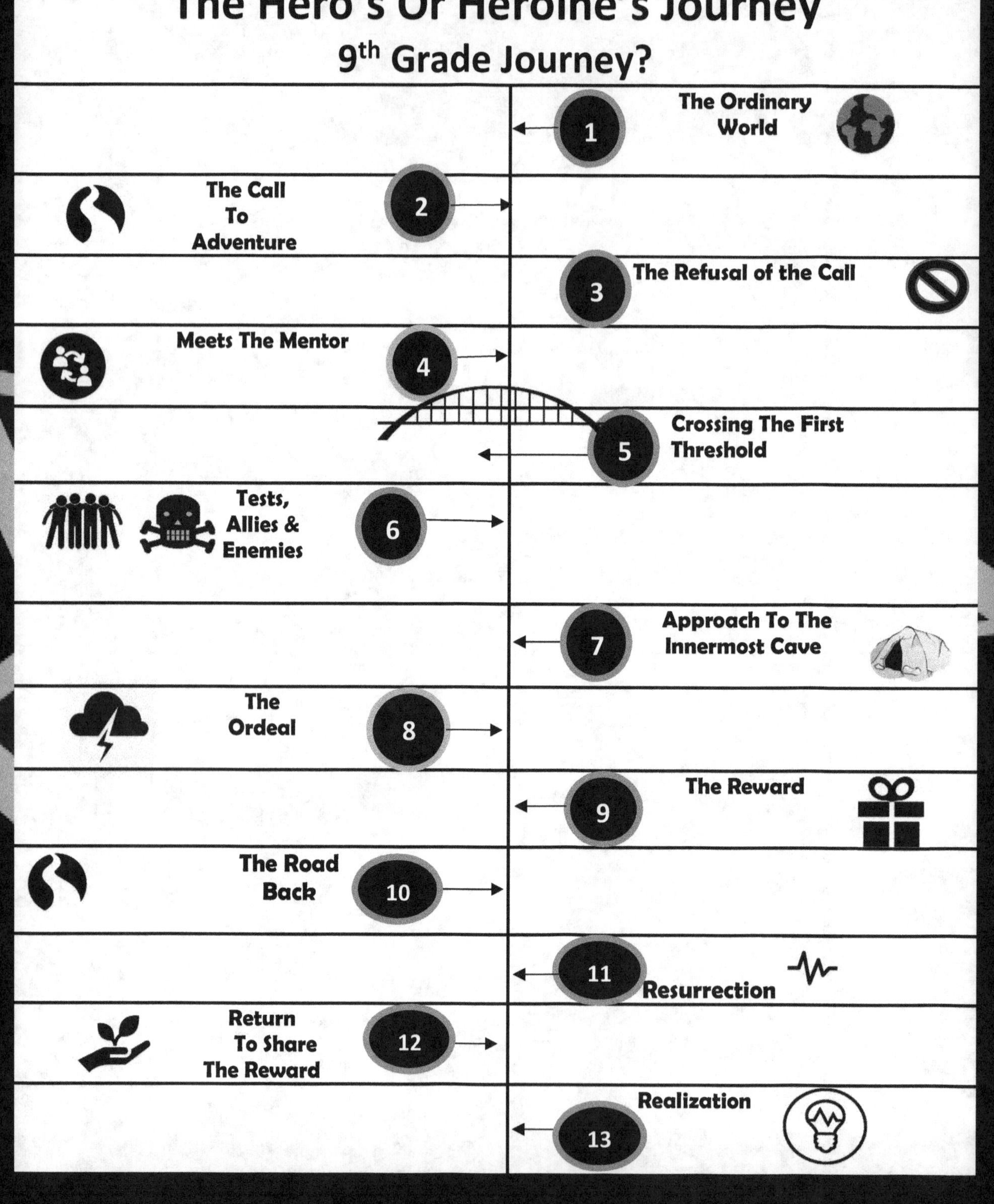
The Hero's Or Heroine's Journey
9th Grade Journey?
1
The Ordinary World
2
The Call To Adventure
3
The Refusal of the Call
4
Meets The Mentor
5
Crossing The First Threshold
6
Tests, Allies & Enemies
7
Approach To The Innermost Cave
8
The Ordeal
9
The Reward
10
The Road Back
11
Resurrection
12
Return To Share The Reward
13
Realization

What Do You See?

What was the major theme for the year?

What Rewards Can You Take With You To The Next Year?

What was your 9th grade version of your archetype?

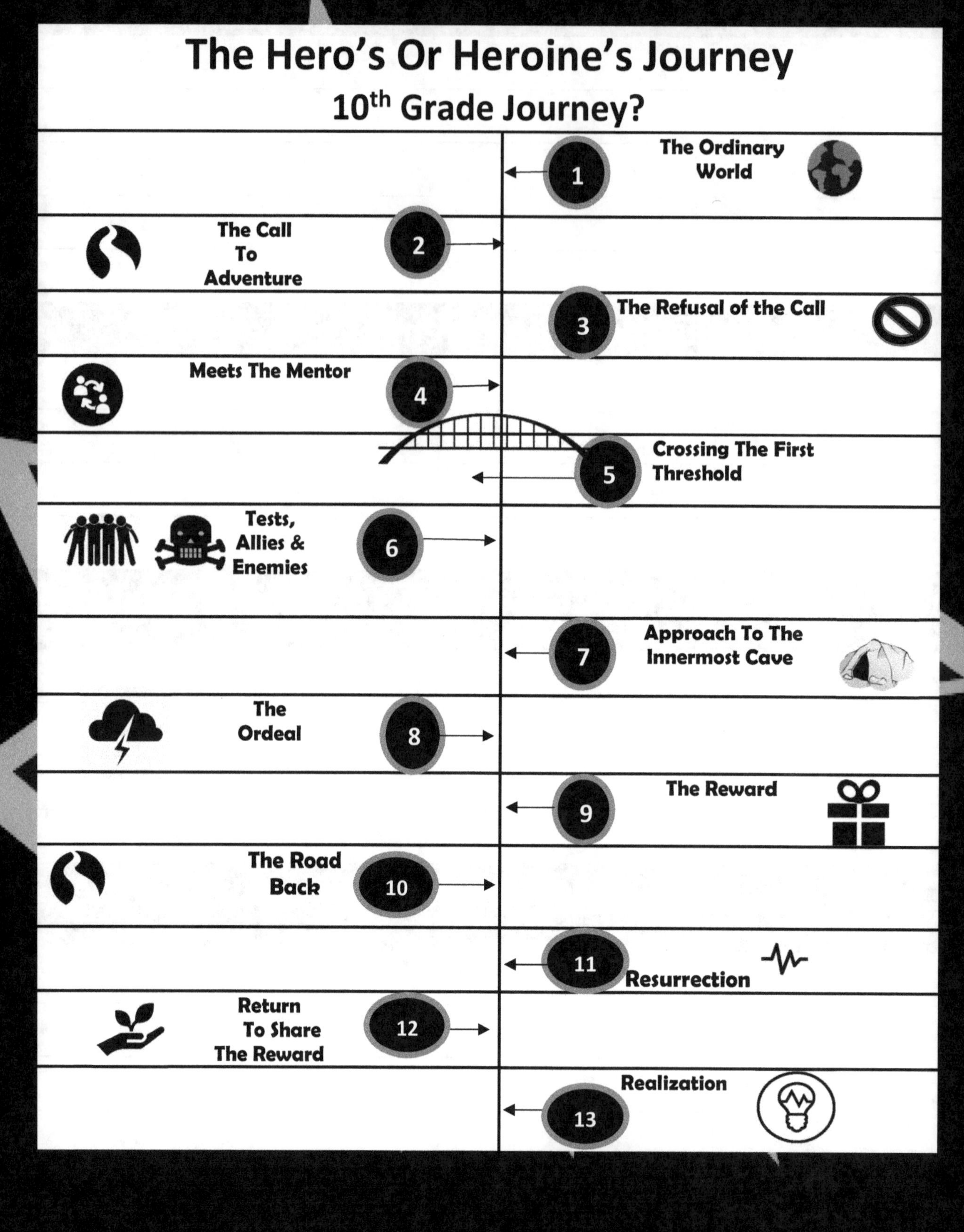
The Hero's Or Heroine's Journey
10th Grade Journey?
1
The Ordinary World
The Call To Adventure
2
3
The Refusal of the Call
Meets The Mentor
4
5
Crossing The First Threshold
Tests, Allies & Enemies
6
7
Approach To The Innermost Cave
The Ordeal
8
9
The Reward
The Road Back
10
11
Resurrection
Return To Share The Reward
12
13
Realization

What Do You See?

What was the major theme for the year?

What Rewards Can You Take With You To The Next Year?

What was your 10th grade version of your archetype?

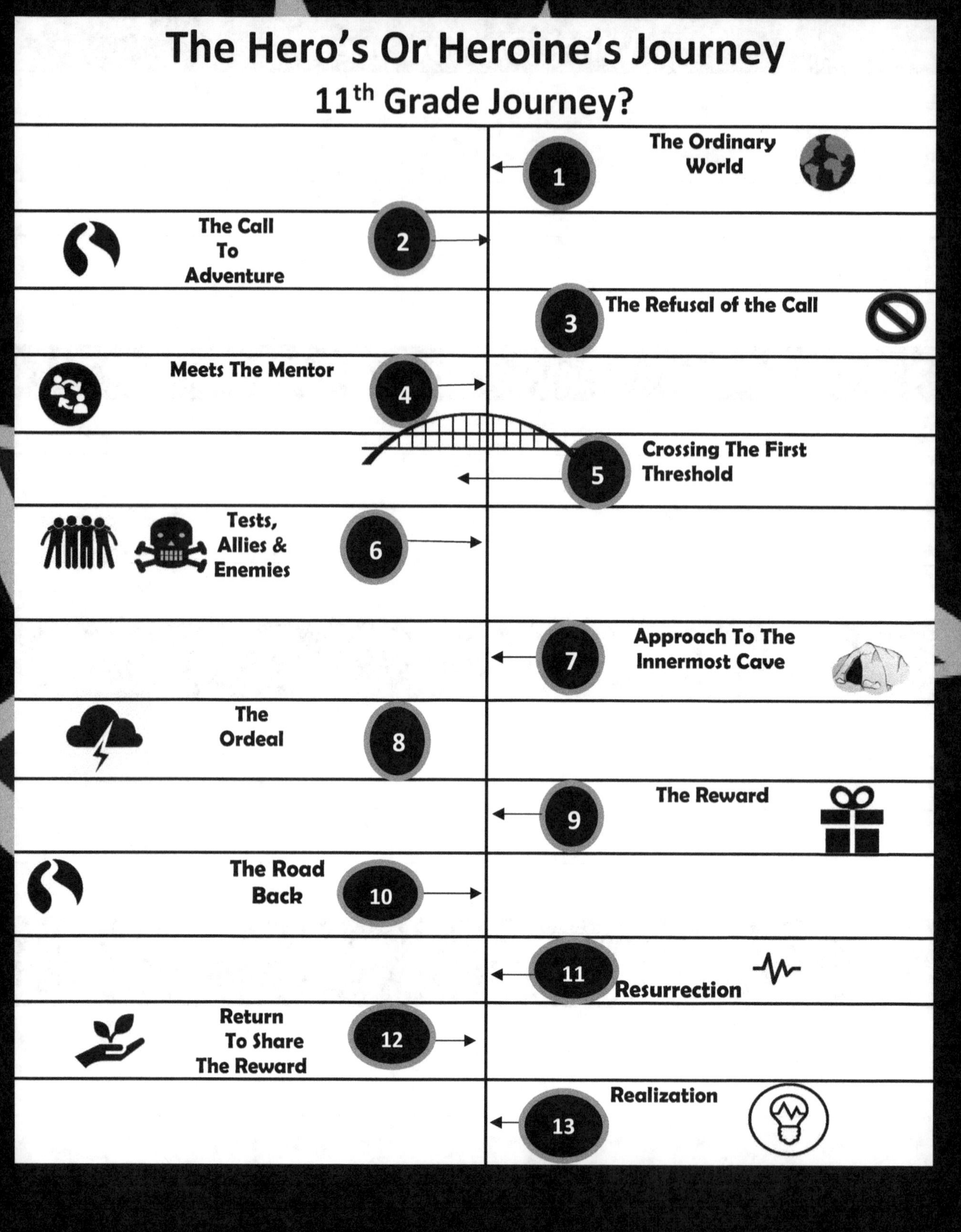
The Hero's Or Heroine's Journey
11th Grade Journey?
1
The Ordinary World
2
The Call To Adventure
3
The Refusal of the Call
4
Meets The Mentor
5
Crossing The First Threshold
6
Tests, Allies & Enemies
7
Approach To The Innermost Cave
8
The Ordeal
9
The Reward
10
The Road Back
11
Resurrection
12
Return To Share The Reward
13
Realization

What Do You See?

What was the major theme for the year?

What Rewards Can You Take With You To The Next Year?

What was your 11th grade version of your archetype?

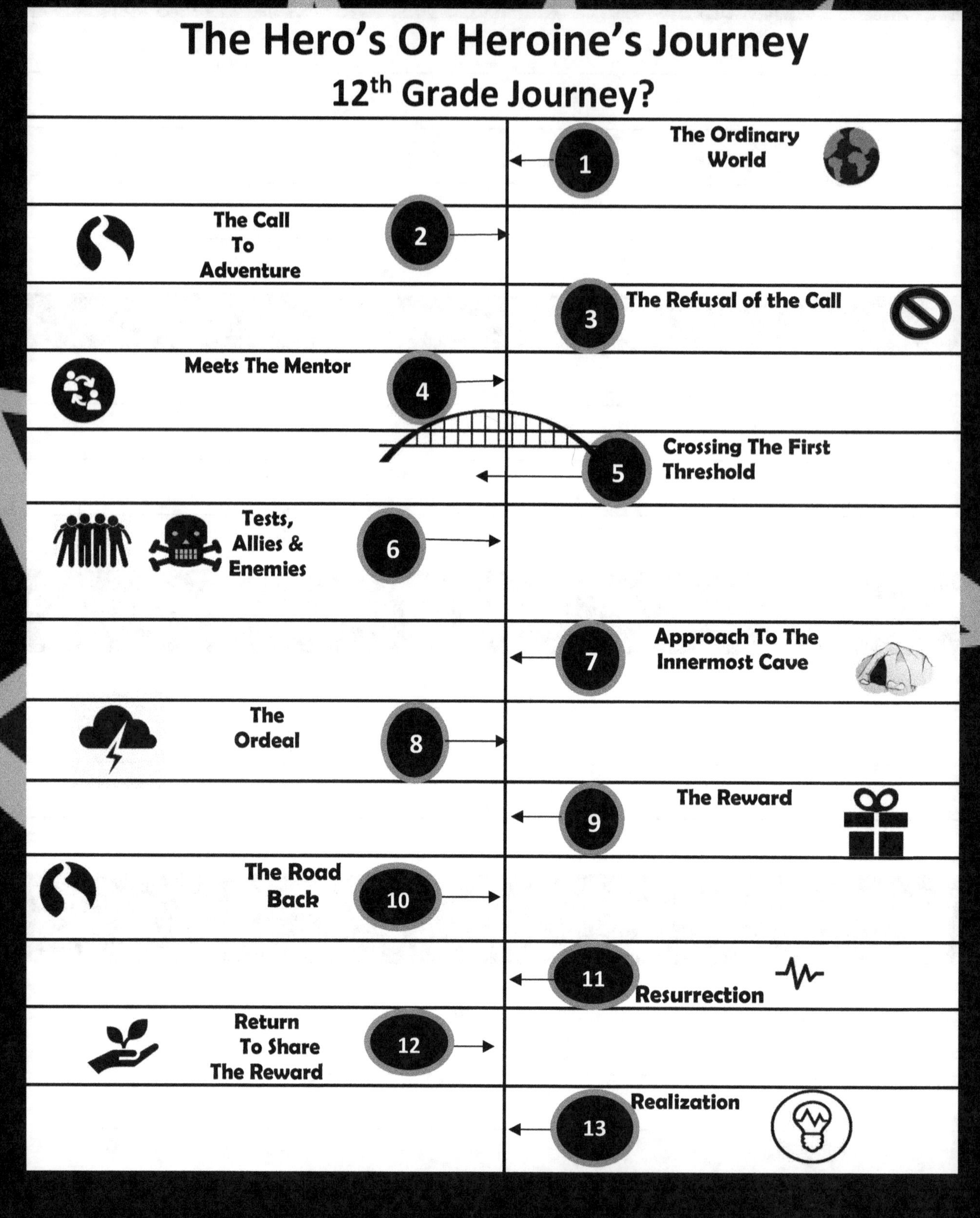
The Hero's Or Heroine's Journey
12th Grade Journey?
1
The Ordinary World
The Call To Adventure
2
3
The Refusal of the Call
Meets The Mentor
4
5
Crossing The First Threshold
Tests, Allies & Enemies
6
7
Approach To The Innermost Cave
The Ordeal
8
9
The Reward
The Road Back
10
11
Resurrection
Return To Share The Reward
12
13
Realization

What Do You See?

What was the major theme for the year?

What Rewards Can You Take With You To The Next Year?

What was your 12th grade version of your archetype?

"

BECOMING

We are all somewhere between our lowest possibility & highest actuality.

With every transition or milestone in life, you, Rising Purpose Peep, are exchanging one possibility for another.

With every transition or milestone in life, you, Rising Purpose Peep, are moving towards your greatest impact through your type of

SUPER."

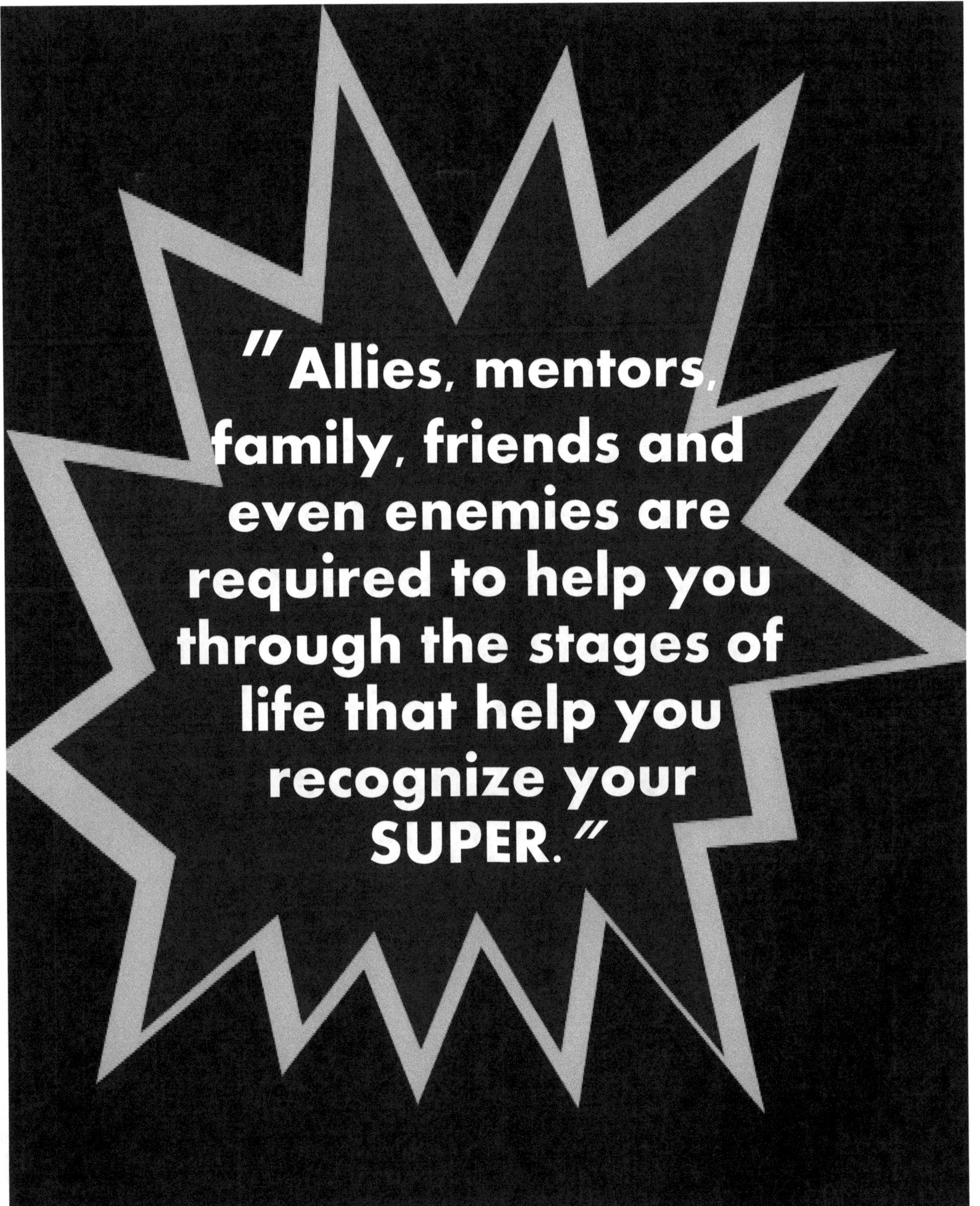
"Allies, mentors, family, friends and even enemies are required to help you through the stages of life that help you recognize your SUPER."

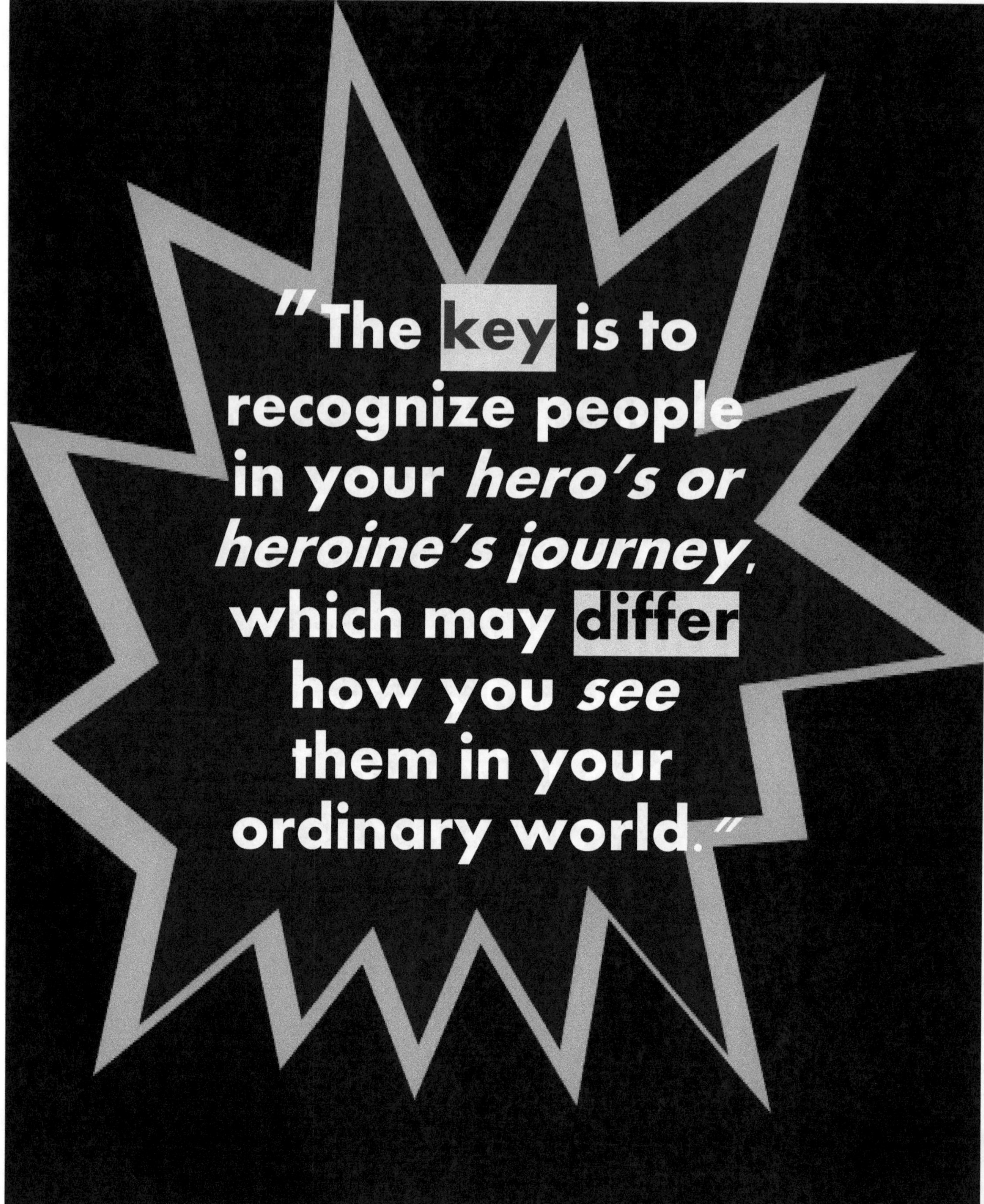
"The key is to
recognize people
in your *hero's or*
heroine's journey,
which may differ
how you *see*
them in your
ordinary world."

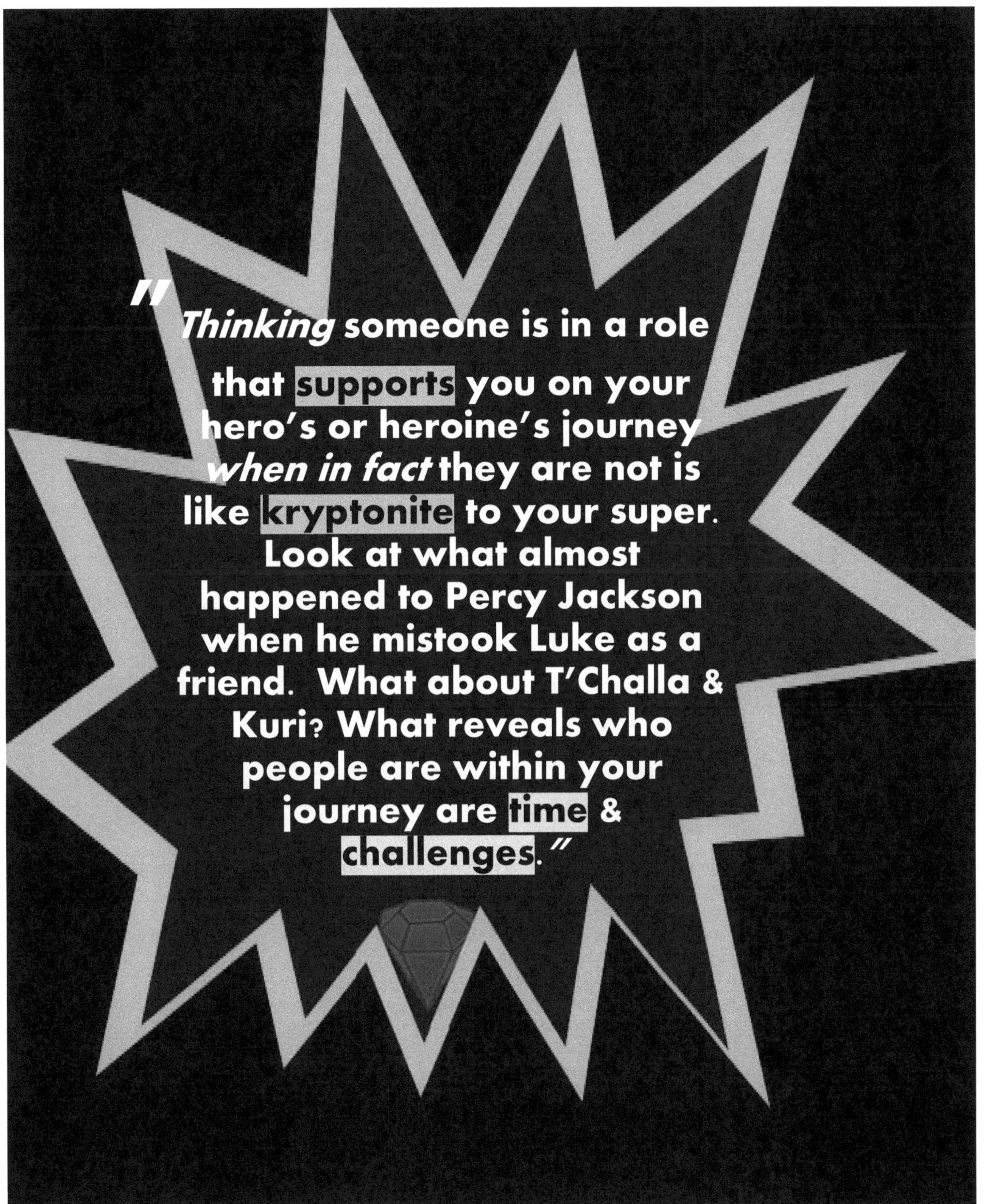
"*Thinking* someone is in a role that supports you on your hero's or heroine's journey *when in fact* they are not is like kryptonite to your super. Look at what almost happened to Percy Jackson when he mistook Luke as a friend. What about T'Challa & Kuri? What reveals who people are within your journey are time & challenges."

Super Orbit Questionnaire

Name	Ally, Enemy, Friend, Frenemy, or Mentor	How Do You Feel In Her/His Presence? Expansive, Small, Etc.	After 90 Days	Experience During a Challenge, Shift or Change?	After Another 90 Days	Experience During a Challenge, Shift or Change?

Ally	Shares the same goal or mission with you. When the mission is over, the relationship may be over
Enemy	Shows up either/and against you or what you show up or take a stand for
Friend	Cares for you personally, you have things in common and shows up for you even when he or she may not agree with what you stand for
Frenemy	A friend who strongly disagrees with your direction or what you stand for
Mentor	Believes in you and your general possibility or in a specific area and because of that shares, guides, shares wisdom or tools to help move you along to your goals

Super Tips:

- ✓ Complete from the perspective of you on your hero's or heroine's journey. Sometimes people relate to you differently when you are changing than when you are in the ordinary world.
- ✓ If people reveal they cannot hang during times of challenge, cool, do not expect them to and just chill with them. Everyone needs people they can come back to from adventures and just chill.
- ✓ Sometimes the most impactful change is in how we relate to people and not expecting more from them than they can give.
- ✓ You can complete your Posse Inventory at the beginning or end of each grade.
- ✓ If there is a difference between what you think and what you feel in your body, go with what you feel in your body.

Super Orbit Exercise

Complete this exercise from the perspective of you and what you understand about your super! This is the version of you that is in the center. Your orbiting relationships surround you from most personal to least personal. The enemy is in the outer orbit, furthest from you because the energy and intention of this person(s) is like kryptonite for your emerging super, right now. Things can change and yet the decisions you make NOW impact whether your super flourishes and matures or diminishes and dies out.

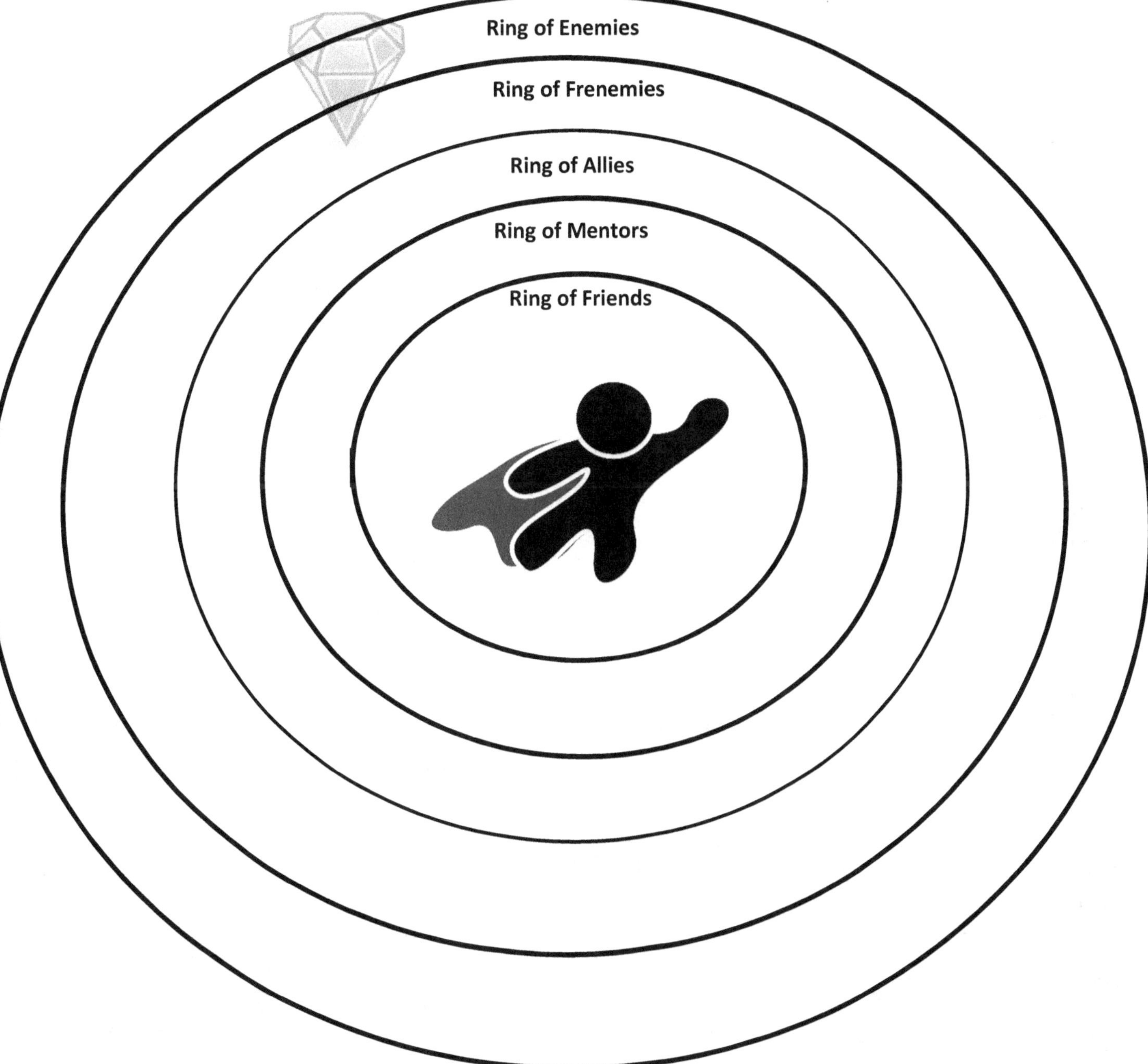

Super Tips:

- ✓ **You'll know you need to reevaluate your Super Orbit when you feel the need to shrink, pressure to go back to an older version of yourself, or sometime of unease in the orbit's closets to your super.**
- ✓ **You'll know you could reconsider your outer rings when the person has proven a shift in against you or for a common goal or purpose. This person *may* be open to consideration to enter the ally orbit. *As soon* as the goal or mission is accomplished, you could reevaluate.**
- ✓ **As you experience relationships in the outer rings of your Super Orbit, you will feel weaker, less energetic, less confident, nervous or on guard. Check in and see if you need any adjustments on how you're spending your time.**

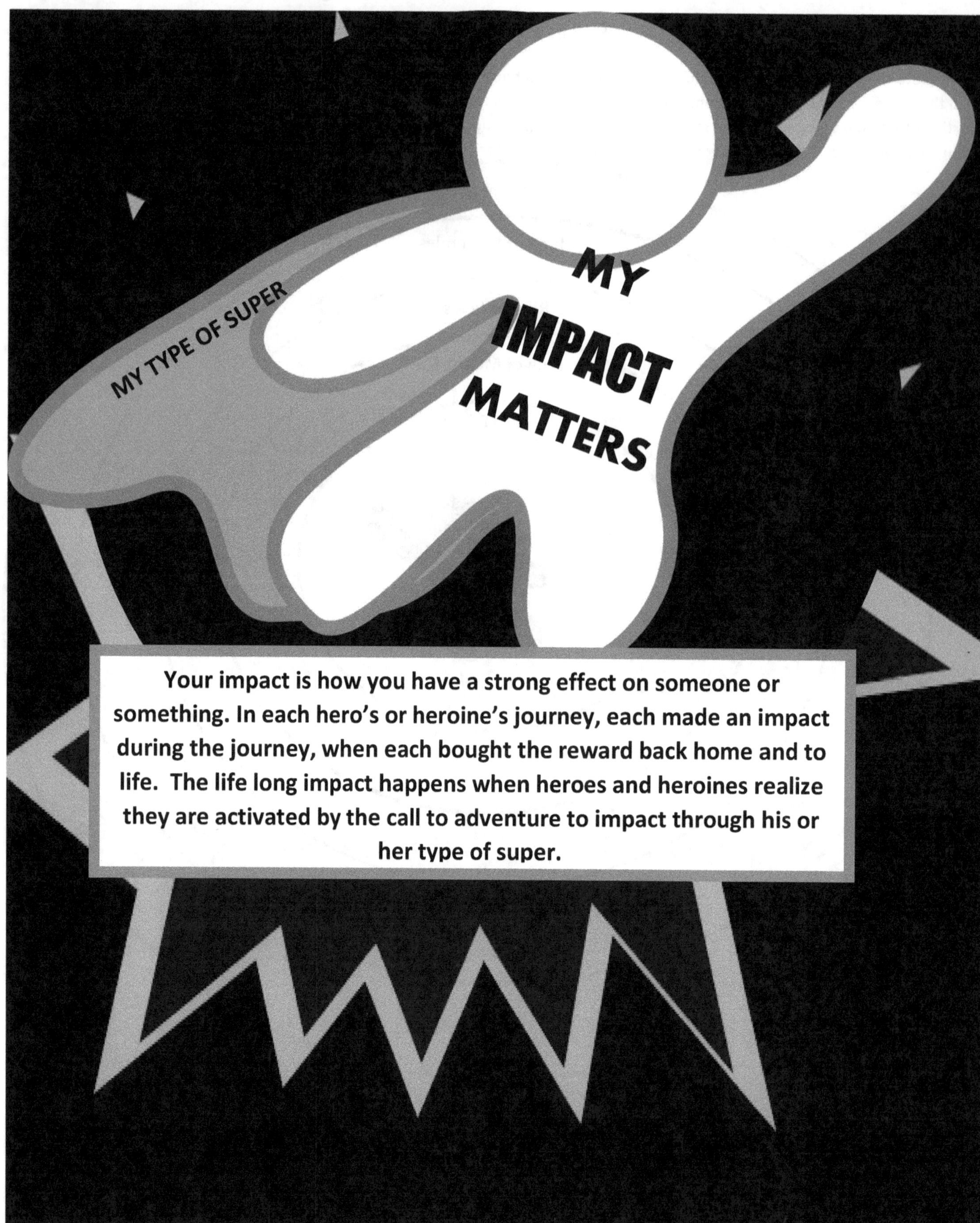
MY TYPE OF SUPER
MY
IMPACT
MATTERS
Your impact is how you have a strong effect on someone or something. In each hero's or heroine's journey, each made an impact during the journey, when each bought the reward back home and to life. The life long impact happens when heroes and heroines realize they are activated by the call to adventure to impact through his or her type of super.

Journey	Impact During The Journey	Impact Bought Back To The Ordinary World	Realization

Your Favorite Movie			
Someone You Respect			
Family Member			
Friend			
Mentor			
YOUR Journey			

Being Super – Impact Reflection

Reflecting on your hero's or heroine's journey, how did you initially refuse your call to action? What were your objections?

Where their previous times you did not accept the call to adventure? What was that like?

Could you imagine yourself, saying yes, next time and what that experience would be? Describe it.

Heroes and heroines are ordinary people that do extraordinary things, making their type of impact through their type of super.

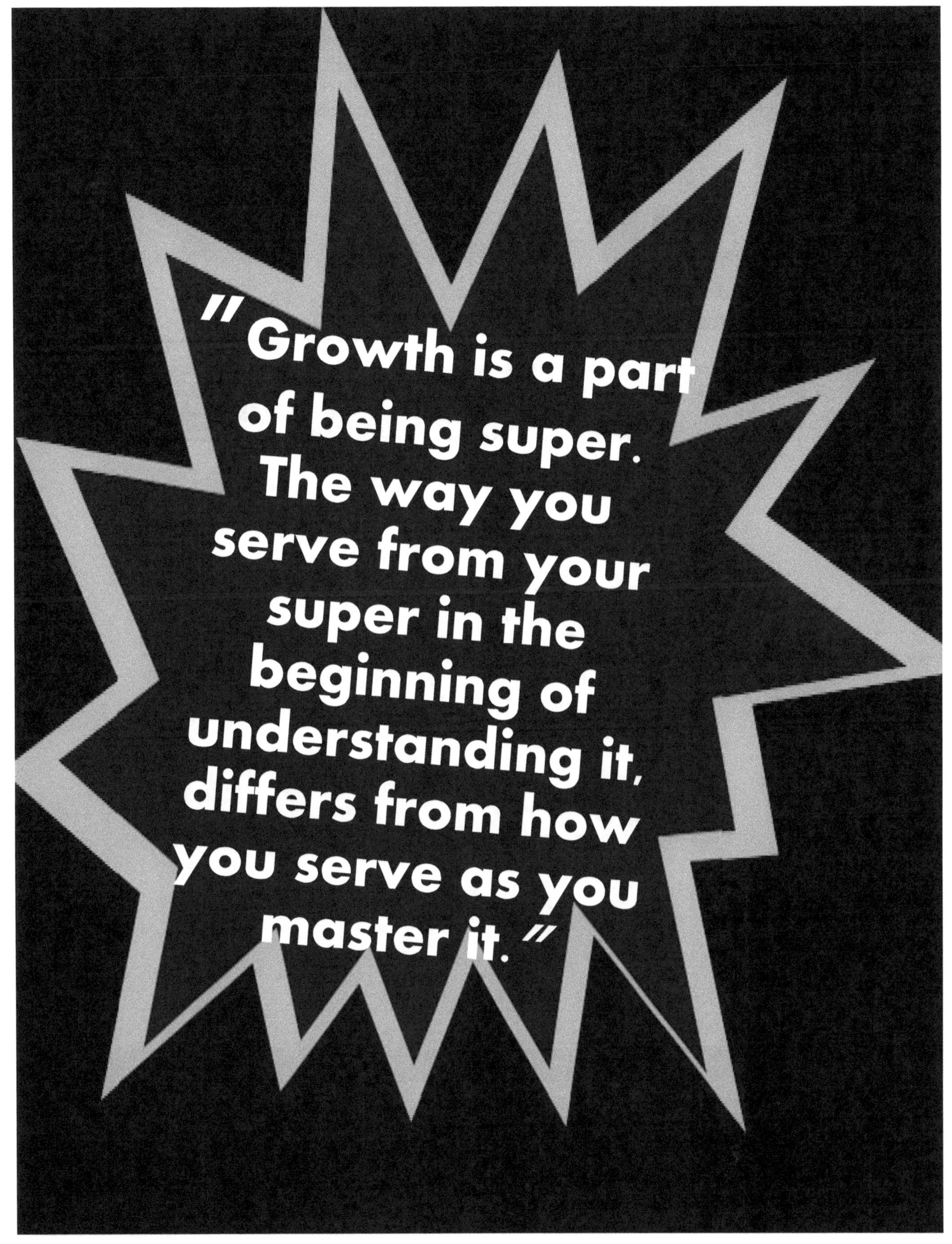
"Growth is a part of being super. The way you serve from your super in the beginning of understanding it, differs from how you serve as you master it."

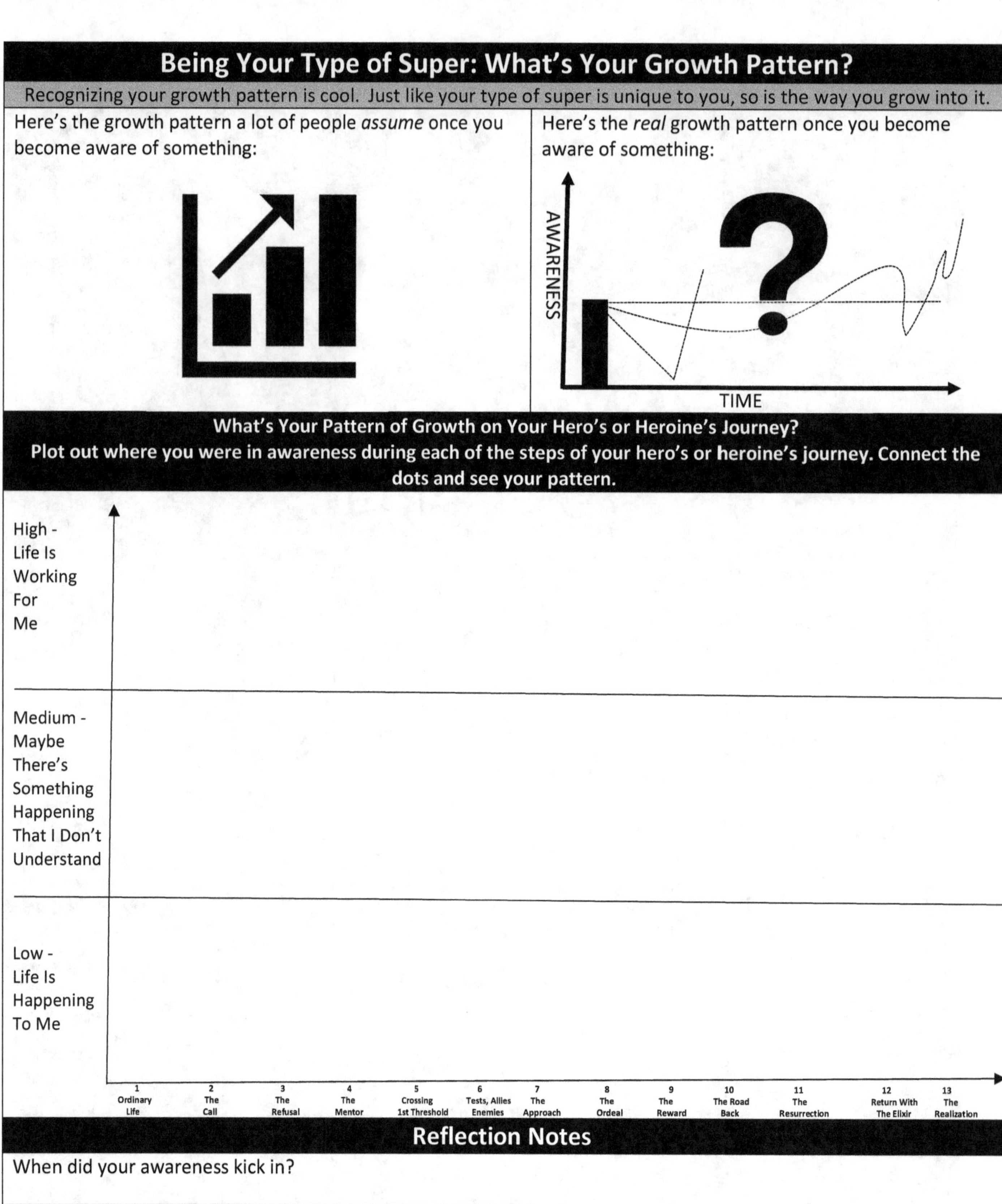

Reflection Notes

When did your awareness kick in?

When did your awareness weaken?

When did your awareness return?

When did your awarness strengthen?

Complete This…

When I experience

______________________________, or

When your awareness kicked in…

______________________________,

When your awareness weakened…

or

____

When your awareness returned…

I will check in because it could be signaling needed steps on my Hero's or Heroine's Journey to understand My Type of Super before

______________________________.

When your awareness strengthened…

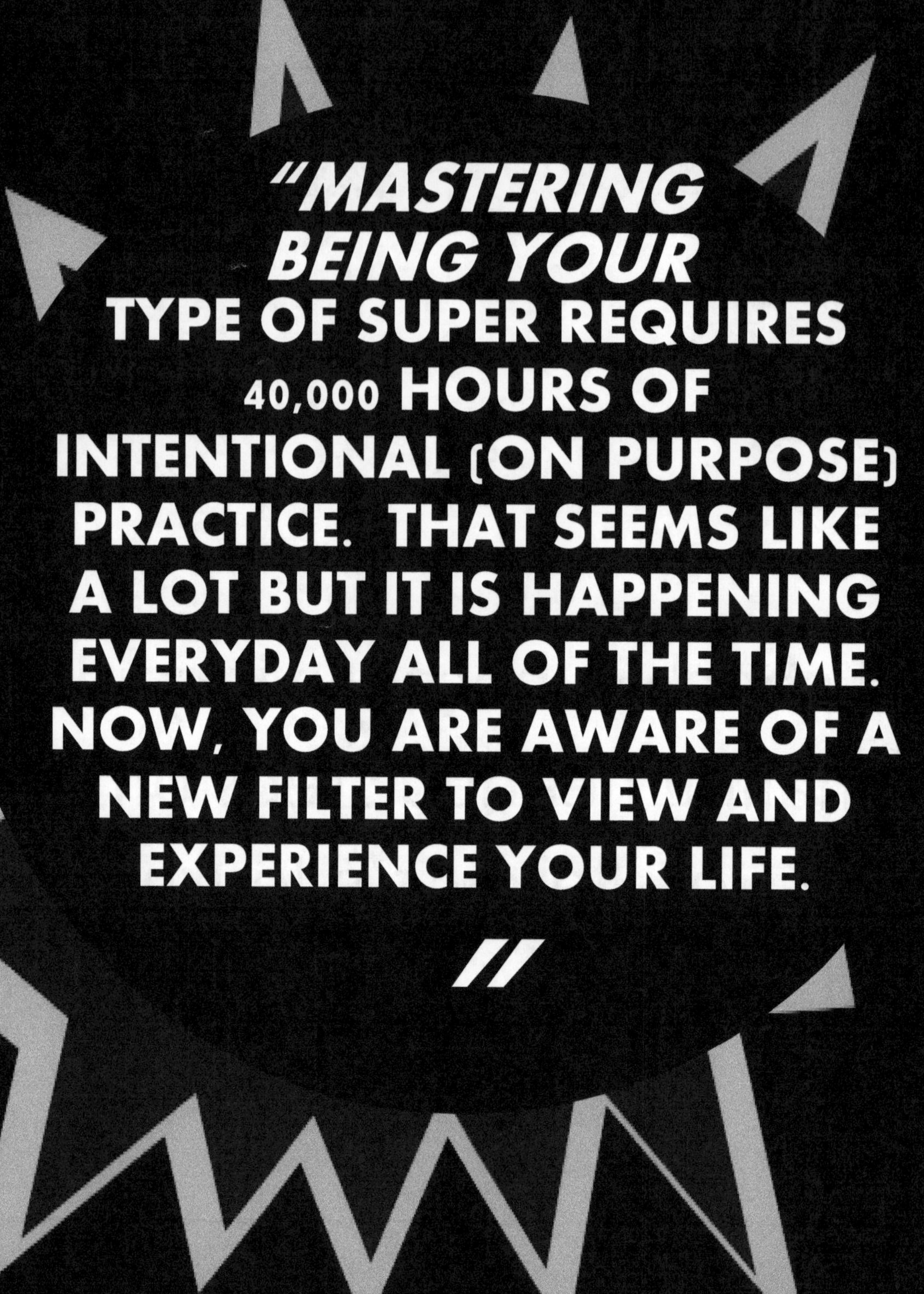
"MASTERING
BEING YOUR
TYPE OF SUPER REQUIRES
40,000 HOURS OF
INTENTIONAL (ON PURPOSE)
PRACTICE. THAT SEEMS LIKE
A LOT BUT IT IS HAPPENING
EVERYDAY ALL OF THE TIME.
NOW, YOU ARE AWARE OF A
NEW FILTER TO VIEW AND
EXPERIENCE YOUR LIFE.
"

Riddle Me This...How Do You Tackle a 40,000 Hour Elephant?

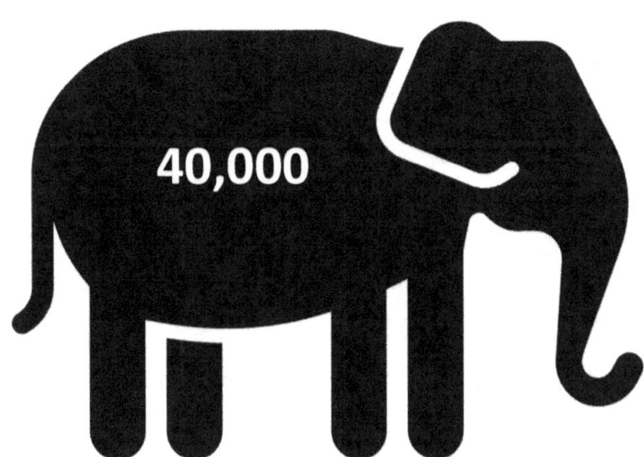

24 Hours At A Time!

Start the day with the intention to be your type of super.

End The Day With a 5 Minute Review of the Day. If there are missed opportunities to express your super, imagine yourself making choices aligned with your type of super. Next time, do it!

BEING

You must be the change you want to see in the world.”

Gandhi

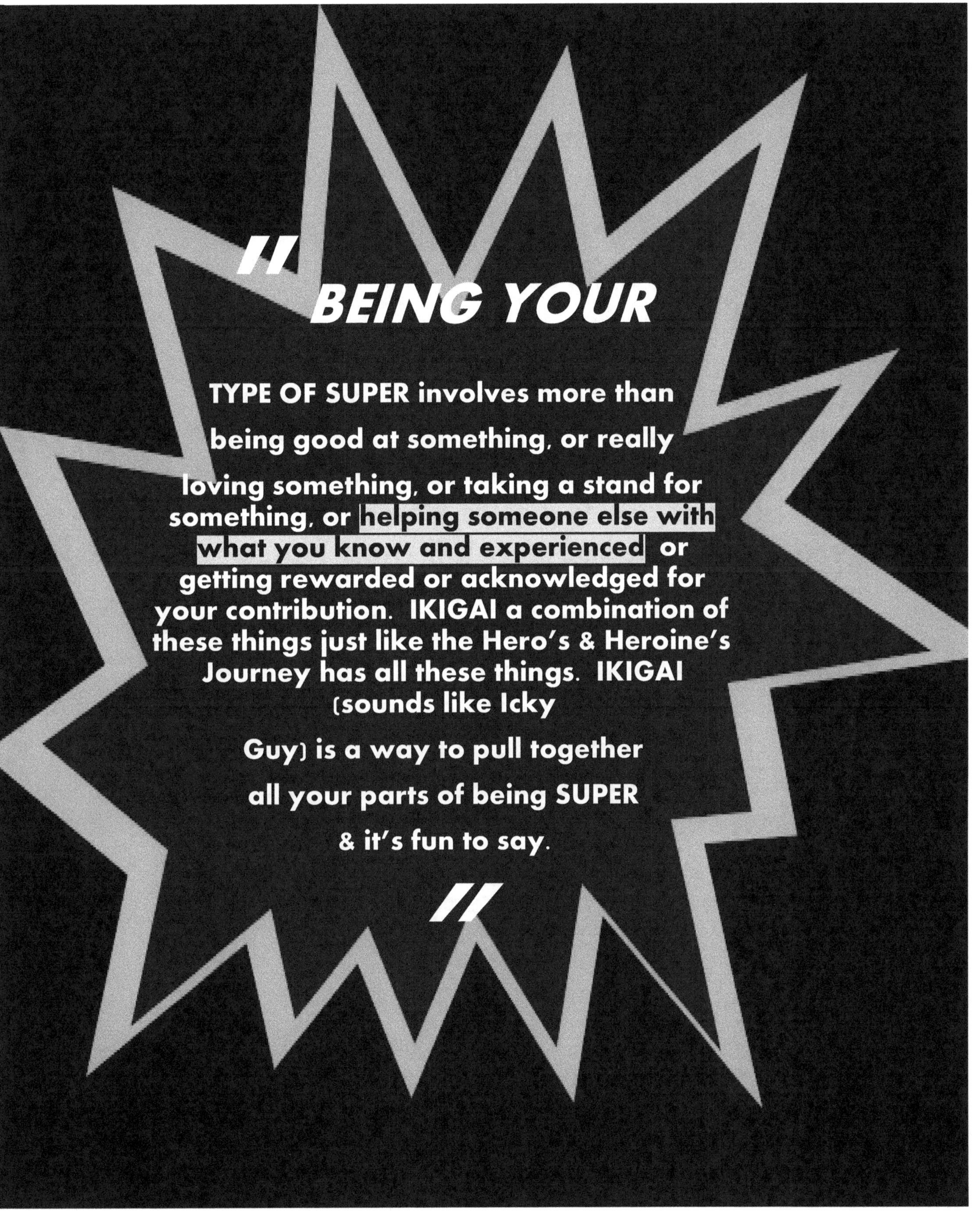
"
BEING YOUR
TYPE OF SUPER involves more than
being good at something, or really
loving something, or taking a stand for
something, or helping someone else with
what you know and experienced or
getting rewarded or acknowledged for
your contribution. IKIGAI a combination of
these things just like the Hero's & Heroine's
Journey has all these things. IKIGAI
(sounds like Icky
Guy) is a way to pull together
all your parts of being SUPER
& it's fun to say.
"

"

IKIGAI

is thousands of years old from two Japanese words translated to valuable living. The Purpose Peeps who practice combining four ways of being with the way they are super call it their reason for being. Think of a Venn Diagram with 4 Circles and in the center of the four circles is IKIGAI. What if when we are out of balance with one area of IKIGAI, then a call to adventure begins to help us to see it—it's usually not obvious. Followed by all the situations, events and people that guide and push us to change, *if we accept the call.*

"

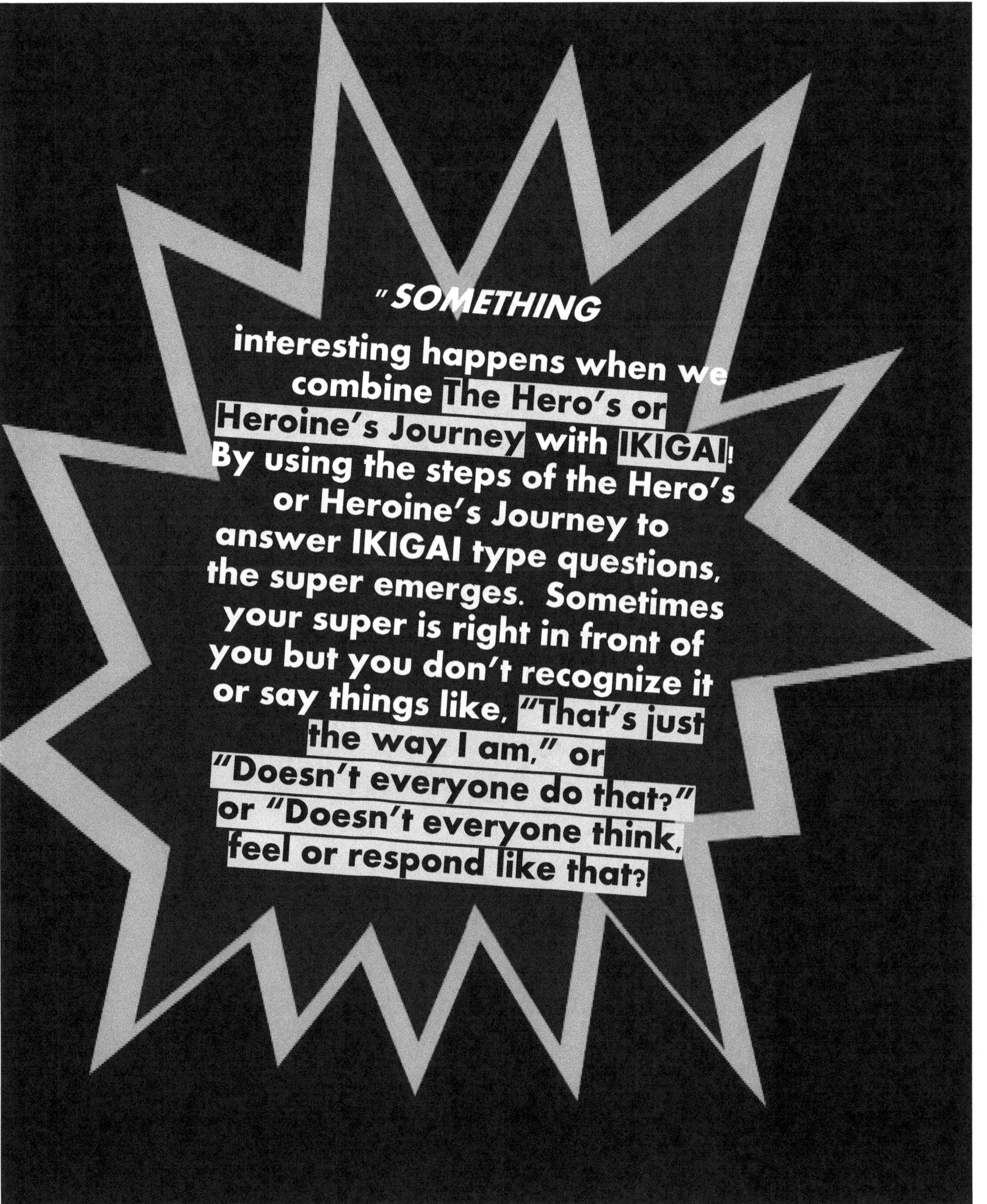
"SOMETHING
interesting happens when we
combine The Hero's or
Heroine's Journey with IKIGAI!
By using the steps of the Hero's
or Heroine's Journey to
answer IKIGAI type questions,
the super emerges. Sometimes
your super is right in front of
you but you don't recognize it
or say things like, "That's just
the way I am," or
"Doesn't everyone do that?"
or "Doesn't everyone think,
feel or respond like that?

"
Although our journeys differ,
we are all filling in the answers to
what we love and will stand for,
what our gifts and talents are
, what the world needs from us &
how we are grounded through
recognition &reward for our contributions.
"

IKIGAI Questions

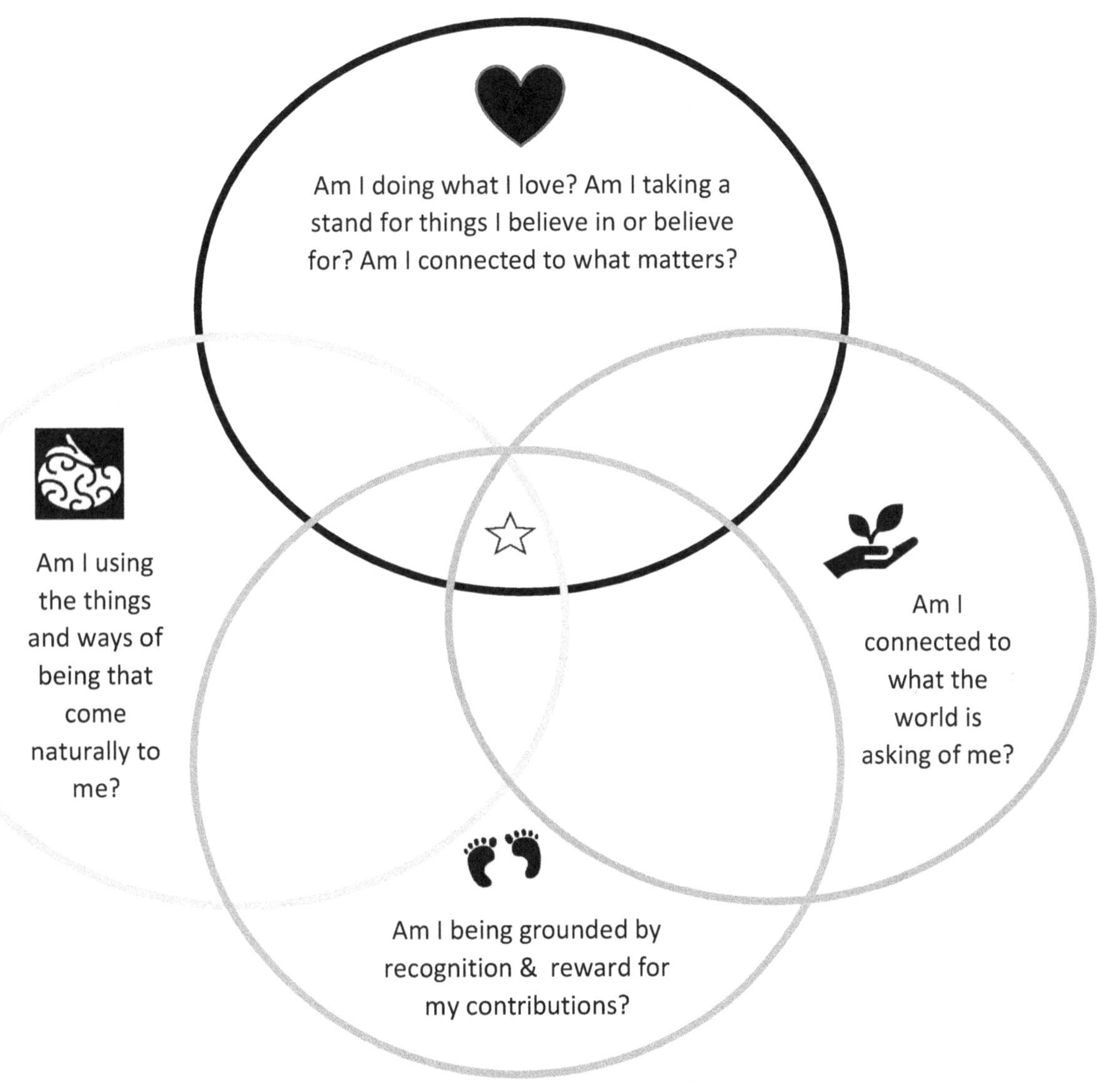

Examples of IKIGAI

What You Love:

- Being (kind, courageous, generous, adventurous, creative, structured, scientific, innovative, compassionate, cooperative, active, healthy, balanced, expressive, reserved, unique, authentic, etc.)
- Being With (any noun including type of person or group, thoughts, experiences)
- Doing (any verb) Most people start here but it's last on purpose!

Gifts & Talents Are You Wired With:

- What do you do well without really having to put a lot of thought into it?
- What are you doing when you completely lose track of time?
- What do you have that you generously share with others?
- What gifts have you received on your journey that you can take back to others?

Your Ordinary World Is Asking For:

- Qualities you posses
- Unique value you bring
- Innovation from your gifts/talents/experiences
- Solutions from your gifts/talents/experiences
- Wisdom from gifts/talents/experiences

You Are Grounded Through Recognition & Reward:

- You are fulfilled in what you do
- You grow in character, wisdom & skillset
- Opportunities/Synchronicity appear
- Solutions from your gifts/talents/experiences
- You are compensated for what you do
- You are a valued member of a tribe

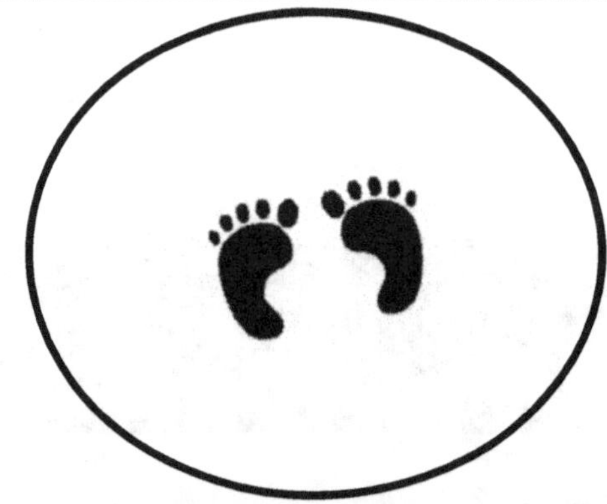

IKIGAI Transitional Areas

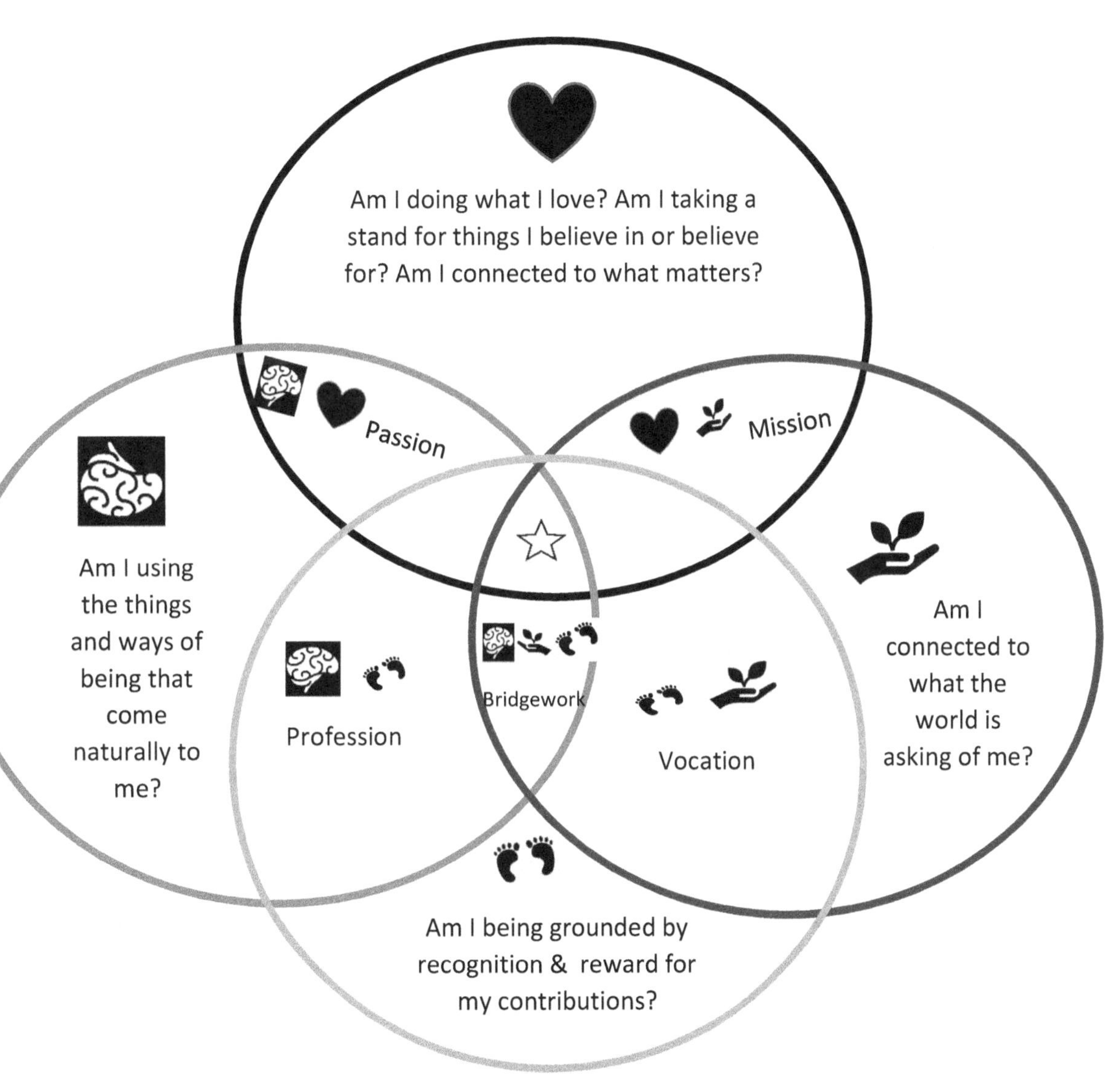

Doing Super: Transitional Areas That Surround IKIGAI

PASSION

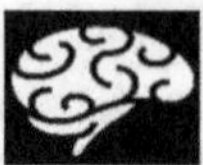 

You have both a love for this and a gift and talent for it. This is what you do just because you love it. This is the call from your soul. It may be a hobby.

HOBBIES, EXTRACURRICULAR ACTIVITIES, FAMILY TRADITIONS, HEALTH WELLNESS, FITNESS

MISSION

You have a love for this and there is a need in the world from this. You may not receive a reward other than fulfillment from serving others and it may not require your gift or talent to do it.

VOLUNTEERING, COMMUNITY SERVICE HOURS, MENTORING

PROFESSION

You Have a Talent/Gift In This Area, There is Grounding (Helps Sustain You), It Does Not Necessarily Have The Pull of What The World Needs From You Or What You Love

CONSIDERATIONS FOR MAJORS, TRADE SCHOOL, ENTREPRENEURSHIP

VOCATION

The World Needs This, There Is Grounding (Helps Sustain You In Some Way) But It Doesn't Reflect Your Gift or What You Love Or Stand For

TUTORING, PART-TIME JOB, BABYSITTING, REPETITIVE TASKS

BRIDGEWORK

Have Talent/Gift To Do, The World Needs This, There Is Grounding (Helps Sustain You) But You Don't Love It Or Have A Heart Connection To It

SIDE HUSTLES, CREATIVE IDEAS TO "BRIDGE" THE GAP TO MORE HEART CENTERED DOING

Understanding what role, the things you do, are offered to do or are planning to do allows you to match your expectation for the experience with the role. And they ALL serve a purpose in moving you closer to IKIGAI. People may get frustrated because they long for IKIGAI without realizing they are close. It's like The Ordeal step in the Hero's or Heroine's Journey, just when they could give up, they breakthrough.

Reflection: What Do You Notice About The Transitional Areas of IKIGAI

Doing Super: IKIGAI Transitional Steps

Fill In Each Section With Current & Future Activities You Are Considering

PASSION

You have both a love for this and a gift and talent for it. This is what you do just because you love it. This is the call from your soul. It may be a hobby.

MISSION

You have a love for this and there is a need in the world from this. You may not receive a reward other than fulfillment from serving others and it may not require your gift or talent to do it.

PROFESSION

You Have a Talent/Gift In This Area, There is Grounding (Helps Sustain You), It Does Not Necessarily Have The Pull of What The World Needs From You Or What You Love

VOCATION

The World Needs This, There Is Grounding (Helps Sustain You In Some Way) But It Doesn't Reflect Your Gift or What You Love Or Stand For

BRIDGEWORK

Have Talent/Gift To Do, The World Needs This, There Is Grounding (Helps Sustain You) But You Don't Love It Or Have A Heart Connection To It

IKIGAI Is Not Perfection But Represents The *EXTRA*ordinary World When Your Inner Super Meets The Needs of the Outer World.

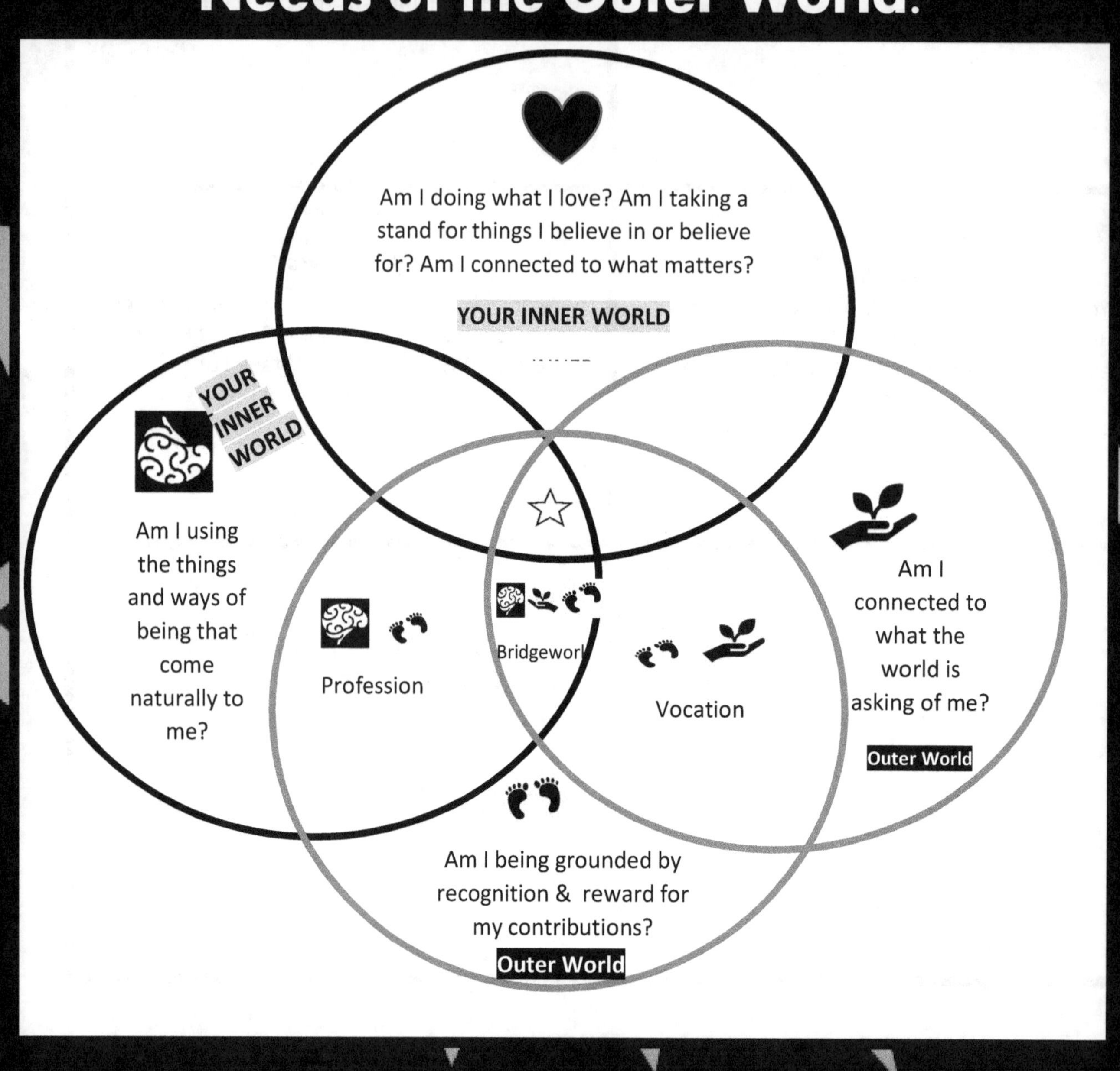

What comes up when you think of EXTRAordinary as bridging your inner super with outer needs?

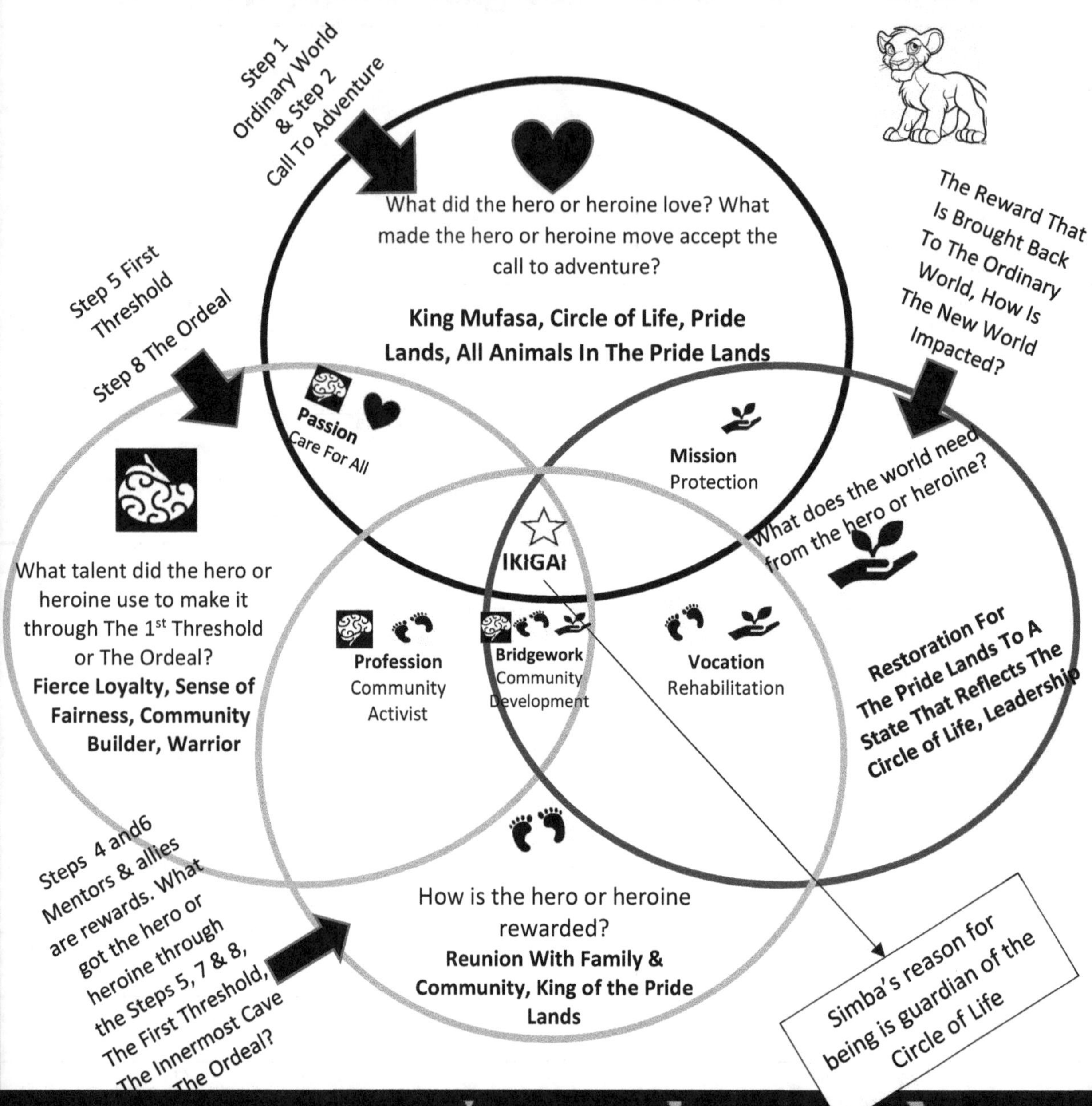
IKIGAI
The Lion King Example
Step 1
Ordinary World
& Step 2
Call To Adventure
What did the hero or heroine love? What made the hero or heroine move accept the call to adventure?
King Mufasa, Circle of Life, Pride Lands, All Animals In The Pride Lands
The Reward That Is Brought Back To The Ordinary World, How Is The New World Impacted?
Step 5 First Threshold
Step 8 The Ordeal
Passion
Care For All
Mission
Protection
What does the world need from the hero or heroine?
What talent did the hero or heroine use to make it through The 1st Threshold or The Ordeal?
Fierce Loyalty, Sense of Fairness, Community Builder, Warrior
IKIGAI
Profession
Community Activist
Bridgework
Community Development
Vocation
Rehabilitation
Restoration For The Pride Lands To A State That Reflects The Circle of Life, Leadership
Steps 4 and6 Mentors & allies are rewards. What got the hero or heroine through the Steps 5, 7 & 8, The First Threshold, The Innermost Cave The Ordeal?
How is the hero or heroine rewarded?
Reunion With Family & Community, King of the Pride Lands
Simba's reason for being is guardian of the Circle of Life

When You Apply IKIGAI To The Story, What Do You See?

How Do Simba's Transition Areas Differ From His IKIGAI?

IKIGAI

Complete Using The Divergent Movie

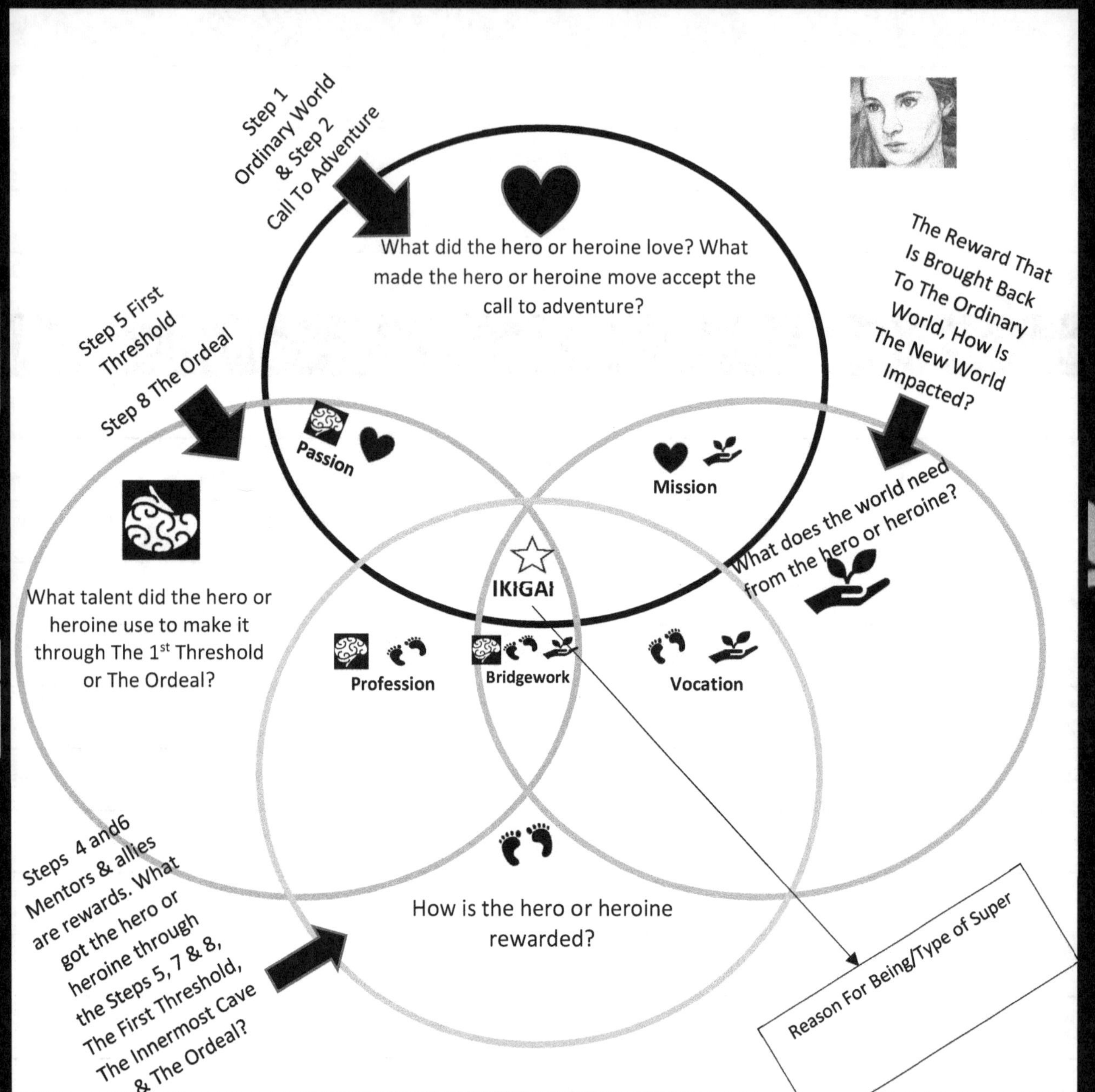

Super Tip: Start with the main circles first (heart, head, feet, hand) then branch out to the transitional areas. Look at the content of your answers within the main circles to create combinations for the transitional areas.

When You Apply IKIGAI To The Story, What Do You See?

IKIGAI

Complete Using The Percy Jackson Movie

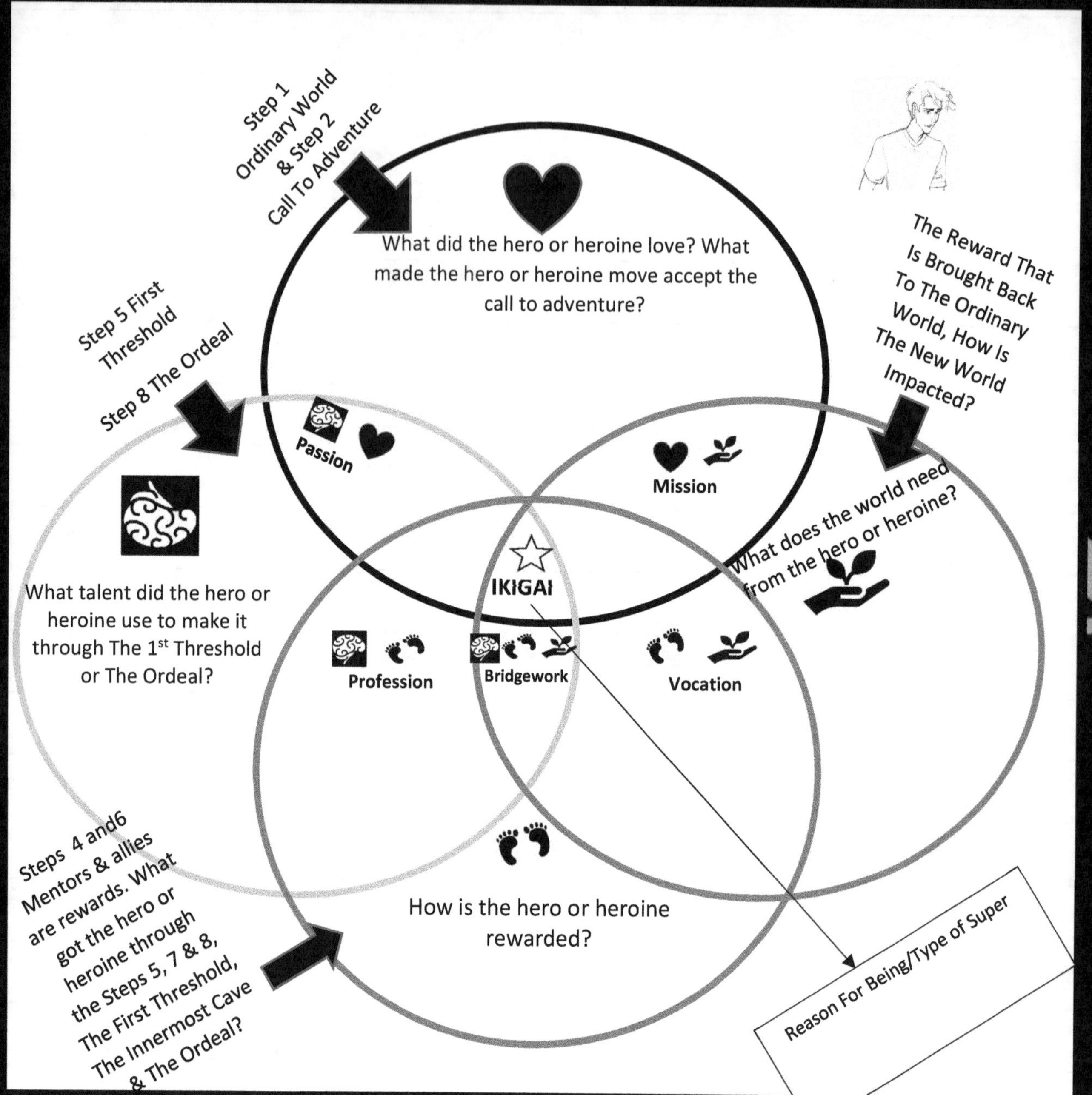

Super Tip: Start with the main circles first (heart, head, feet, hand) then branch out to the transitional areas. Look at the content of your answers within the main circles to create combinations for the transitional areas.

When You Apply IKIGAI To The Story, What Do You See?

IKIGAI

Complete Using The Black Panther Movie

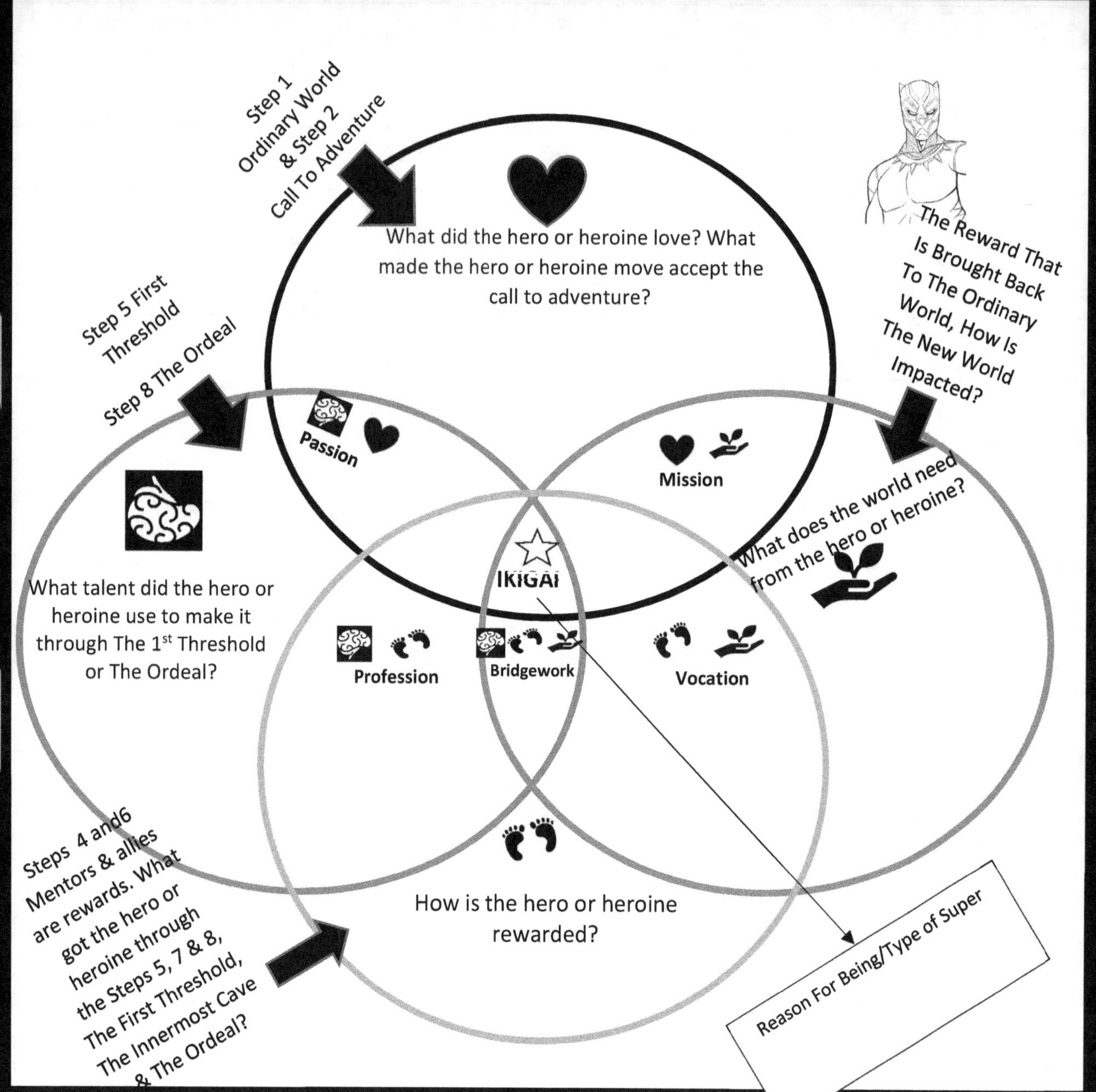

Super Tip: Start with the main circles first (heart, head, feet, hand) then branch out to the transitional areas. Look at the content of your answers within the main circles to create combinations for the transitional areas.

When You Apply IKIGAI To The Story, What Do You See?

IKIGAI

Complete Using The Wonder Woman Movie

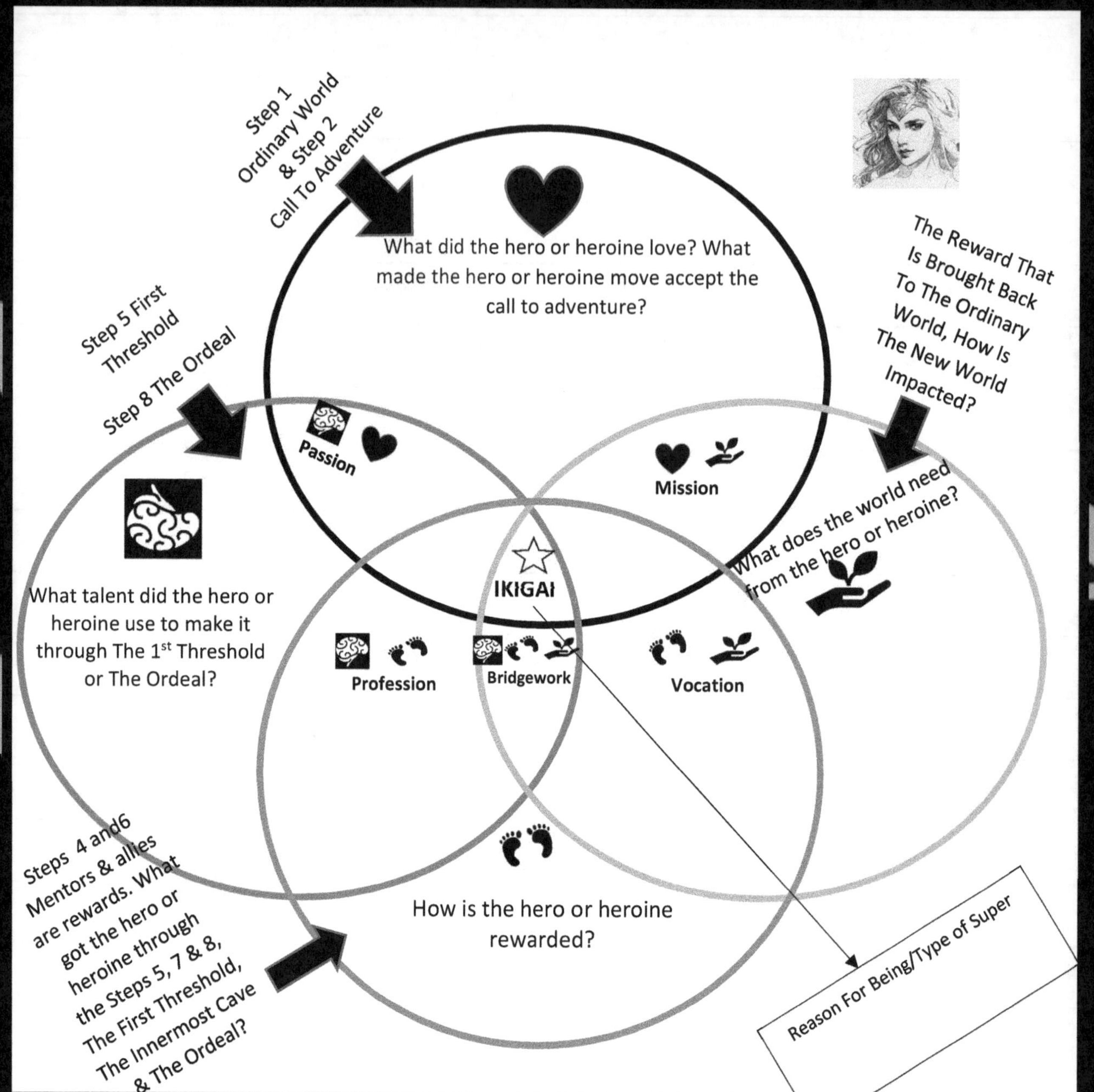

Super Tip: Start with the main circles first (heart, head, feet, hand) then branch out to the transitional areas. Look at the content of your answers within the main circles to create combinations for the transitional areas.

When You Apply IKIGAI To The Story, What Do You See?

IKIGAI

Complete Using Your Hero's Or Heroine's Journey

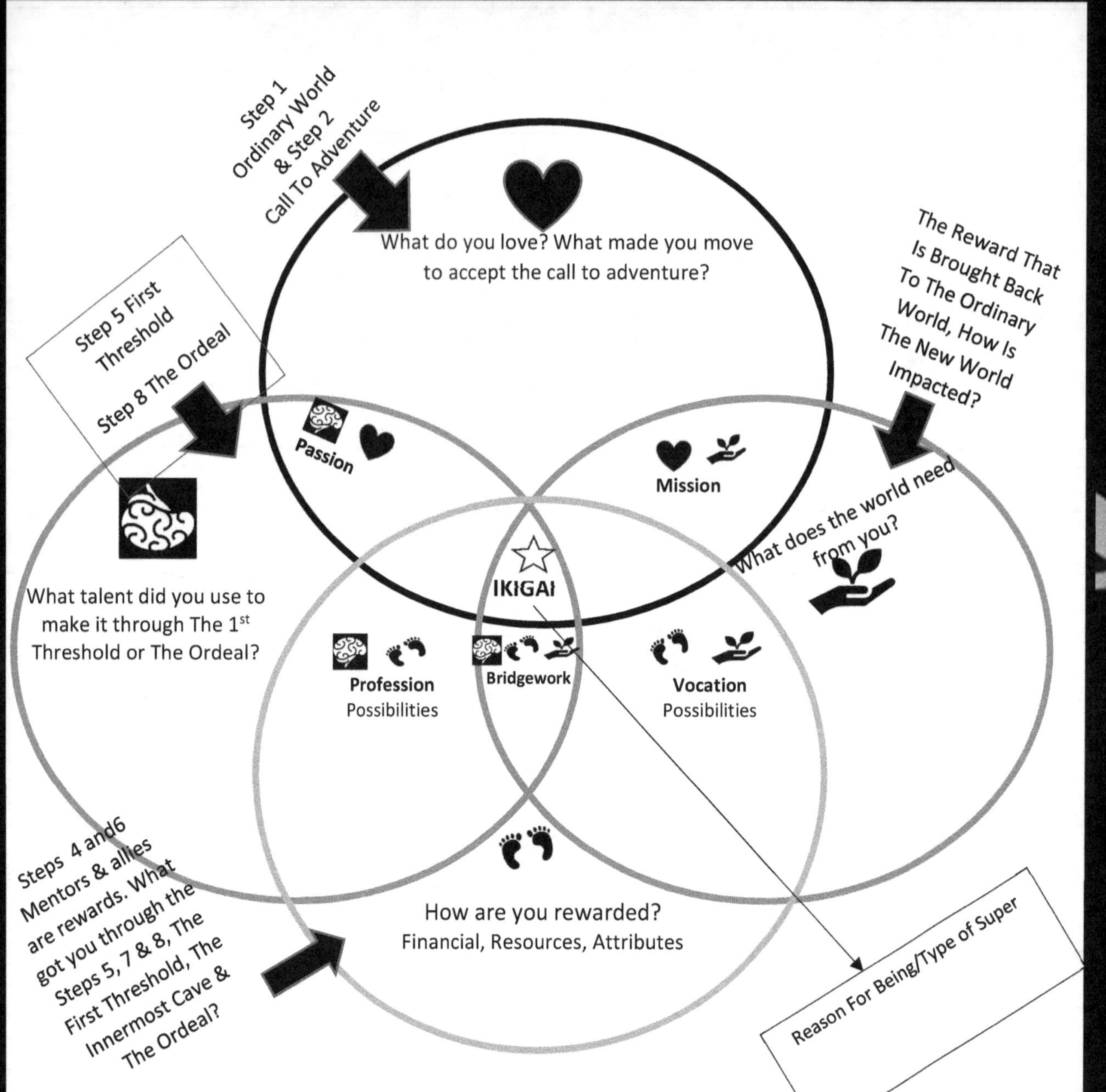

Super Tip: Start with the main circles first (heart, head, feet, hand) then branch out to the transitional areas. Look at the content of your answers within the main circles to create combinations for the transitional areas.

When You Apply IKIGAI To The Story, What Do You See?

How Do YOU Describe Your Reason For Being? Your Type of Super?

How Do Your Top 3 Values (from the beginning exercise) Impact Your Type of Super?

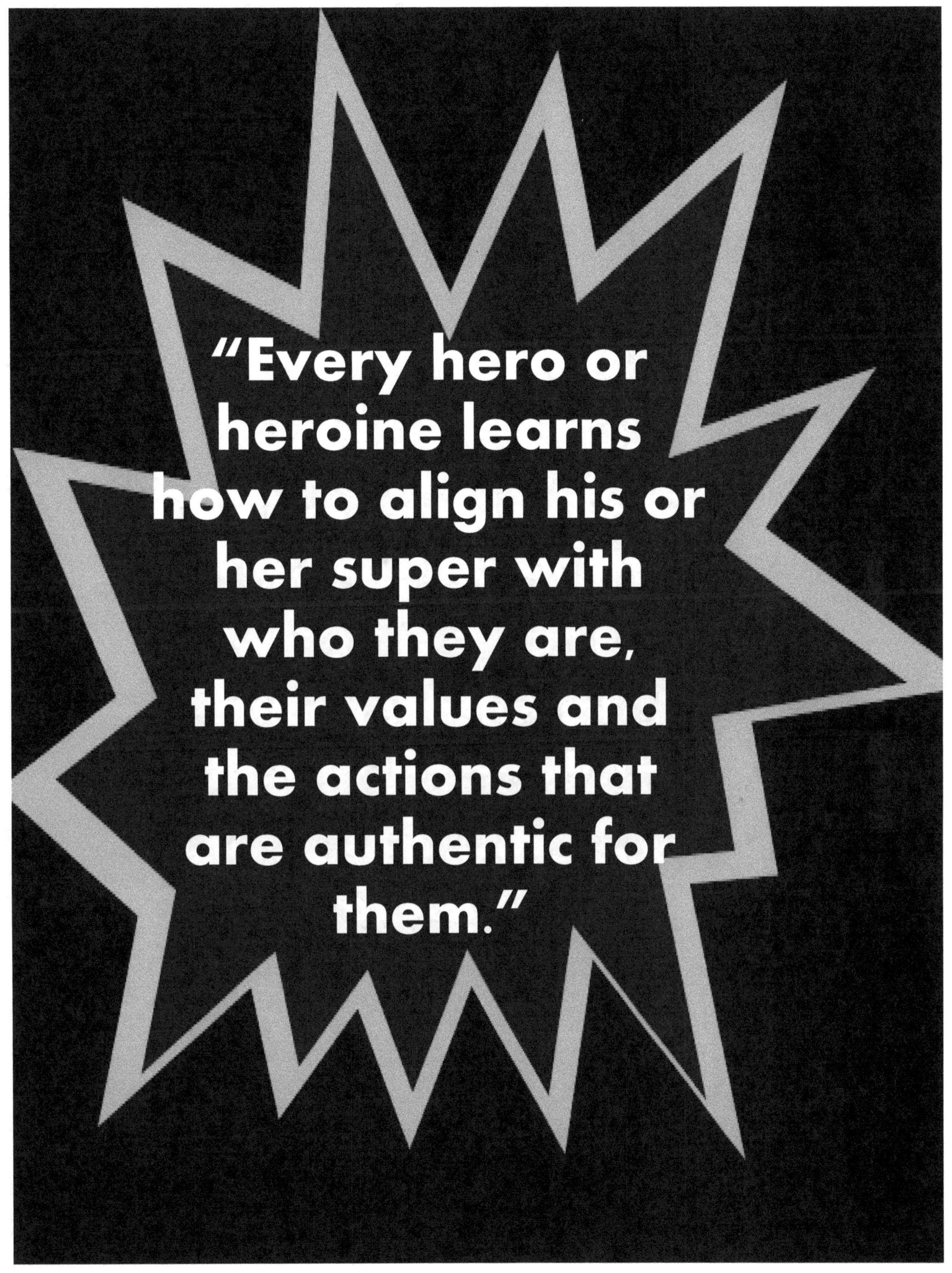
"Every hero or
heroine learns
how to align his or
her super with
who they are,
their values and
the actions that
are authentic for
them."

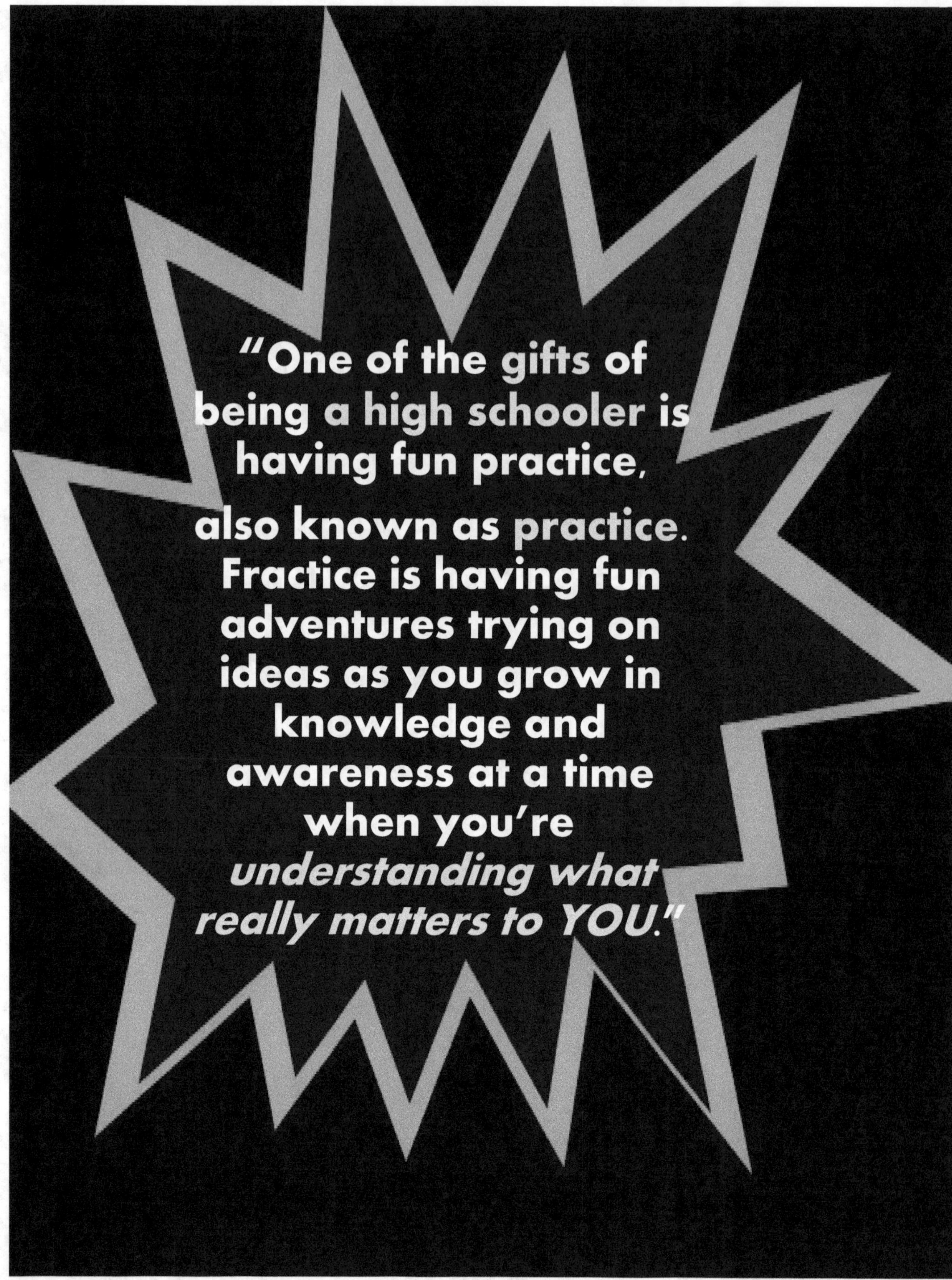
"One of the gifts of
being a high schooler is
having fun practice,
also known as practice.
Fractice is having fun
adventures trying on
ideas as you grow in
knowledge and
awareness at a time
when you're
*understanding what
really matters to YOU.*"

Have a yearly experience with fractice. At the beginning of the year, set an intention with all that you know about your type of super to name it and have experiences with being super. Your yearly reviews show what you are taking into the next year. Be *intentional* (on purpose) about being with your type of super. Answer the questions below and YOLO your fractice.

It's	Freshman Year	20__

My Top 3 Values Are:	My Type of Super Is
1.	
2.	I initially accepted or refused this type of super because:
3.	My super is influenced by these major events:
My Super Orbit Is:	1.
Friends/Allies/Mentors:	2.
Frenemies/Enemies:	3.

	The things I love or take a stand for are:
	My experiences with these people, places or things are:
	I learned:

	I am really gifted at/talented in the area(s) of:
	My experiences in being with this aspect of my type of super are:
	I learned:

	What the world needs from me is/are:
	My experiences with being with my impact are:
	I learned:

	My rewards for rocking out my type of super are:
	My experiences with being rewarded are:
	I learned:

What I liked about this experience:	
What I disliked about this experience:	
How I would choose differently & why:	

	It's	Sophomore Year	20__

My Top 3 Values Are:	My Type of Super Is
1.	I initially accepted or refused this type of super because:
2.	My super is influenced by these major events:
3.	1.
My Super Orbit Is:	2.
Friends/Allies/Mentors:	3.
Frenemies/Enemies:	

	The things I love or take a stand for are:
	My experiences with these people, places or things are:
	I learned:
	I am really gifted at/talented in the area(s) of:
	My experiences in being with this aspect of my type of super are:
	I learned:
	What the world needs from me is/are:
	My experiences with being with my impact are:
	I learned:
	My rewards for rocking out my type of super are:
	My experiences with being rewarded are:
	I learned:
What I liked about this experience:	
What I disliked about this experience:	
How I would choose differently & why:	

	It's	Junior Year	20__

My Top 3 Values Are:		My Type of Super Is
1.		I initially accepted or refused this type of super because:
2.		My super is influenced by these major events:
3.		1.
My Super Orbit Is:		2.
Friends/Allies/Mentors:		3.
Frenemies/Enemies:		

	The things I love or take a stand for are:
	My experiences with these people, places or things are:
	I learned:

	I am really gifted at/talented in the area(s) of:
	My experiences in being with this aspect of my type of super are:
	I learned:

	What the world needs from me is/are:
	My experiences with being with my impact are:
	I learned:

	My rewards for rocking out my type of super are:
	My experiences with being rewarded are:
	I learned:

What I liked about this experience:	
What I disliked about this experience:	
How I would choose differently & why:	

	It's	Senior Year	20__

My Top 3 Values Are: 1. 2. 3.		My Type of Super Is
		I initially accepted or refused this type of super because:
My Super Orbit Is:		My super is influenced by these major events:
Friends/Allies/Mentors:		1.
Frenemies/Enemies:		2.
		3.

	The things I love or take a stand for are:
	My experiences with these people, places or things are:
	I learned:
	I am really gifted at/talented in the area(s) of:
	My experiences in being with this aspect of my type of super are:
	I learned:
	What the world needs from me is/are:
	My experiences with being with my impact are:
	I learned:
	My rewards for rocking out my type of super are:
	My experiences with being rewarded are:
	I learned:
What I liked about this experience:	
What I disliked about this experience:	
How I would choose differently & why:	

SPINNING YOUR WHEEL OF FORTUNE

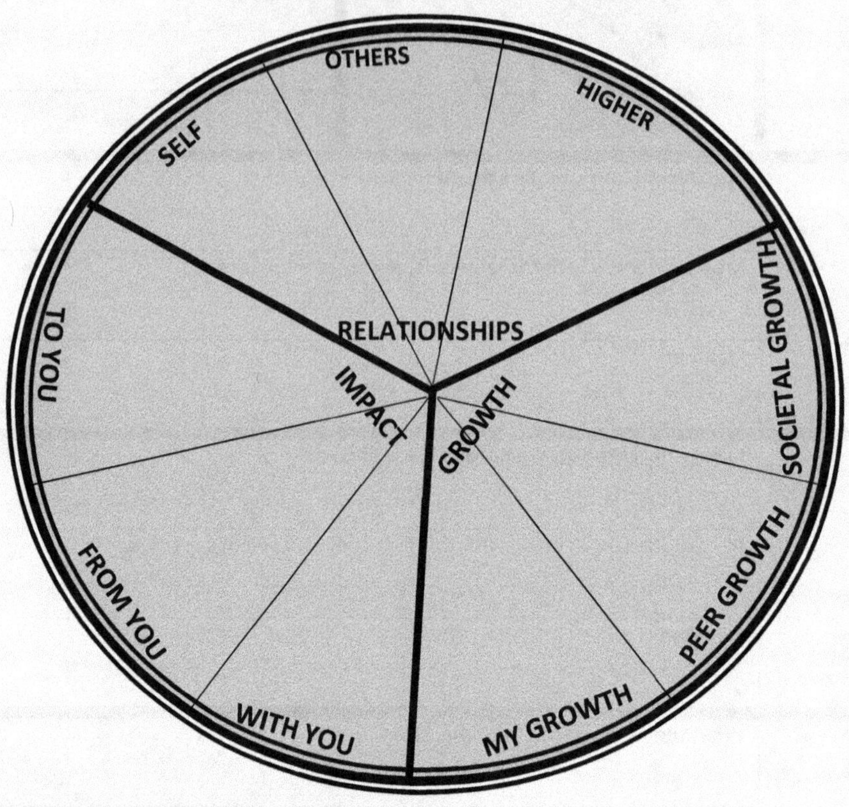

DIRECTIONS: Just Check In	**Here's a quick check in you can do daily, weekly, monthly and yearly. Quickly check into your relationships, impact and growth. How do these areas feel right now from different lenses—from inside of you to extensions from you. For the wheel to rotate smoothly, all aspects of the wheel should be activated.**	Who or what is impacting you? Are you receiving wisdom, insight, inspiration?	IMPACT
		How are you impacting others, the things you love?	
		Are you partnering with other supers to make an impact?	
RELATIONSHIPS	Are you taking care of yourself? How's your self-talk?	Are you growing? What's stopping you?	GROWTH
	Are you connected with others? Are your connections for you?	Are you growing with your allies, friends & through your mentors?	
	Are you connected to something greater than you that grounds you?	Is your growth connected to societal change?	

DOING

"I think a hero is any person really intent on making this a better place for all people.

Maya Angelou

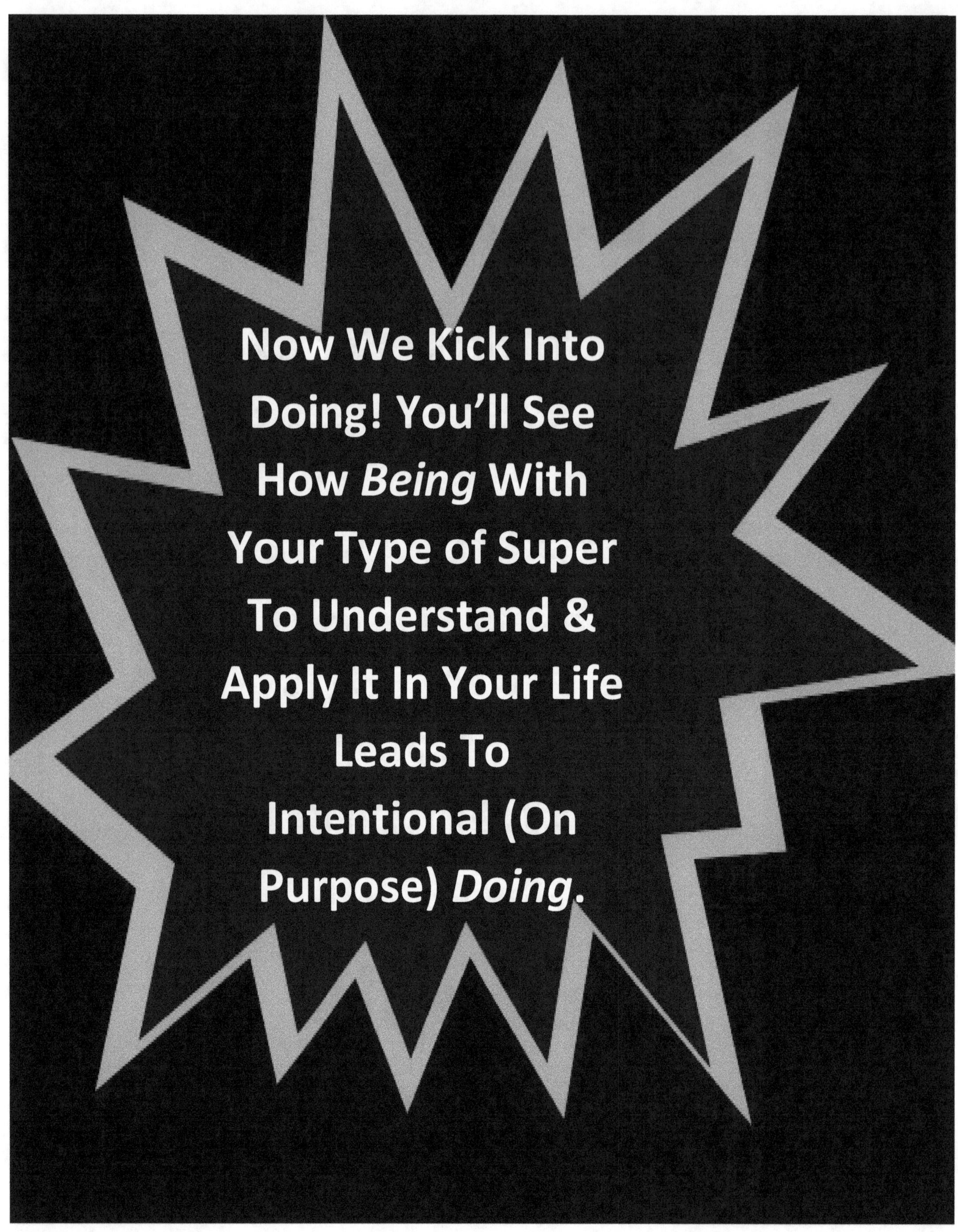
Now We Kick Into
Doing! You'll See
How *Being* With
Your Type of Super
To Understand &
Apply It In Your Life
Leads To
Intentional (On
Purpose) *Doing*.

IKIGAI QUARTERLY CHECK IN

See page 74 for examples of each area.

Am I Living My Heart's Expression?

How Am I Learning More About & Expressing My Gifts & Talents?

Am I Connecting My Type of Super With The Needs of Others?

Am I Seeing Rewards That Ground Me While Living My Type of Super?

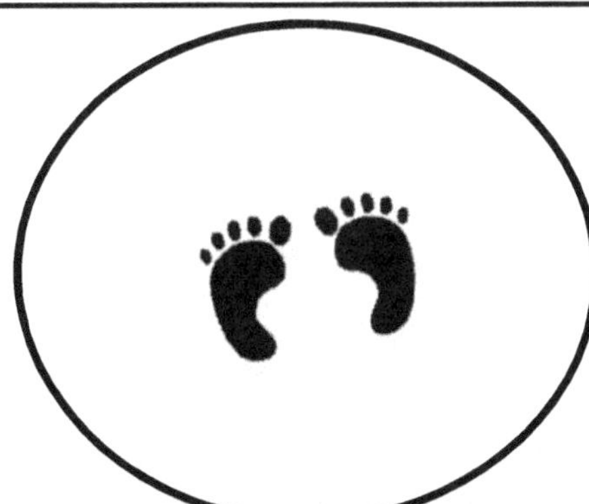

IKIGAI Your Goals

Reminder: IKIGAI Is Not Perfection, It Is Where Your Inner Super & Ordinary World Needs Meet To Have Extraordinary Experiences. Your Transitional Areas Move You Toward IKIGAI. Use Them!

1. Review Your IKIGAI

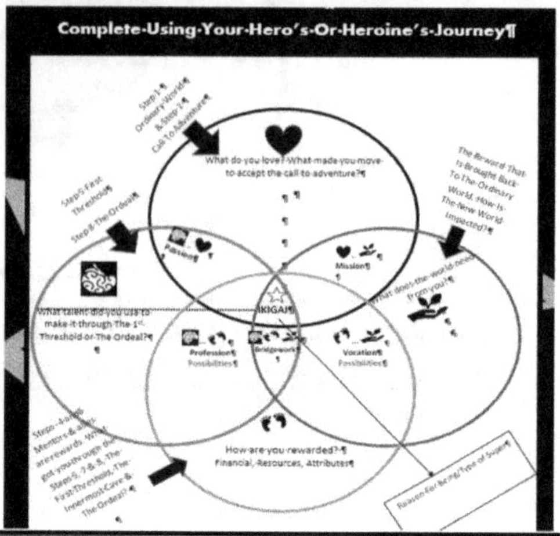

2. Circle The Main Area(s) Where You Have A Lot of Understanding

Look at your current goals and see where they fit in the IGIKAI areas. Set a goal to remain strong in this area. What are your reps that strengthen this area?

3. Circle The Main Area(s) Where You Have Less Clarity

Set a goal to be more tuned in to new info in this area. When your next call to adventure happens, notice how it is building your awareness in one or more of these areas.

Review Your Transition Areas

Passion

Profession

Vocation

Bridgework

As you plan for the future, review where your goals fall in IKIGAI and adjust accordingly. The goal is not perfection but for your inner super to connect with the needs of the ordinary world in a way that rewards you providing grounding for you.

IKIGAI GOAL EXAMPLES

See page 74 for examples of each area.

Am I Living My Heart's Expression?

- Drop One Activity or Club For Another That I Really Love or Feel Strongly About
- Make time for hobbies that I love to do just because
- Spend Time With People I Really Care About

How Am I Learning More About & Expressing My Gifts & Talents?

- Stop Doing Vocational Stuff Outside of My Required Course Work
- Take A Course or Watch You Tube Videos About the Area of My Gifts and Talents
- Join Clubs That Highlight the Areas of My Gifts & Talents

Am I Connecting My Type of Super With The Needs of Others?

- Volunteer at Make A Wish Foundation
- Research Trends About Things I Am Passionate About

Am I Seeing Rewards That Ground Me While Living My Type of Super?

- Choose Activities That Reward My Super Like Shadowing, Interning, Intentional Social Media

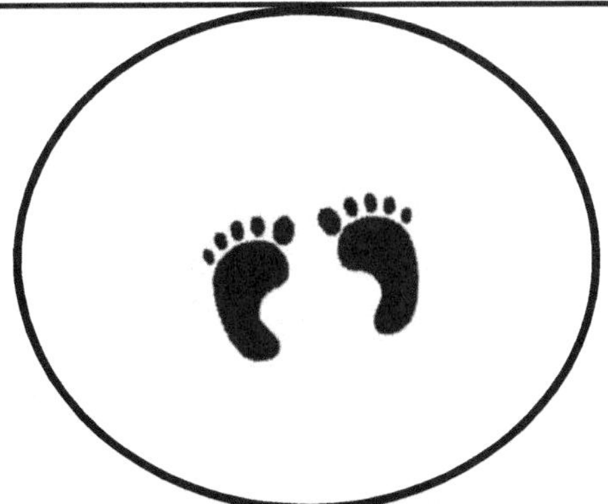

Being Super: How To Unlock & Leverage Your U

When you are connecting your inner super with an outer world opportunity, during the inquiry and interview process, whomever you are meeting with wants to know YOU and know if your super is the *best* match for what they need. You also want to know if the opportunity is a match for your super. Use your U to make it easy for both you and your interview to figure this out!

Your U is a simple version of your hero's or heroine's journey that is in everyday language and not your journey language. You start with where you are now and take them on a quick, journey. That's the inner part of the U. You also perform research to understand the world surrounding your opportunity, that's the outer part of the you. Whenever you write or speak, you want to be sure you to highlight the strongest connections in your U. Here's an example.

CURRENT STATE

At ABC Company, we are passionate about investing in the communities we serve, especially talented youth who are curious about our emerging industry

YOUR CURRENT STATE

I am a Junior at Acme HS, with a talent for graphic design. I am passionate about using my skills to simplify complex terms. This is what I do in my study groups and on my YouTube channel. I love it! Your mentorship program is just the thing to connect me with the latest technology in the field I plan to pursue.

RETURN TO CURRENT STATE WITH REASONS

I am a great candidate because I have initiative and experience bridging art and science for younger students and peers.

REWARD/FEEDBACK

I will consider this student as a strong intern candidate because of her maturity, experience and entrepreneurial spirit. She took the feedback from her high school teacher and ran with it.

CURRENT NEED

DESCRIPTION/MISSION

Next generation of talented designers with a take charge attitude (intern description). Priority is for seniors.

YOUR JOURNEY

I became really sure about my path when I babysat children in my family to help out **(call to adventure)** and I learned ways to make homework, especially math and science, fun and easy to understand **(reward).** My scienc teacher **(mentor)** told me I had a gift and allowed me to create graphics for our cla **ward).**

Being Super: How To Unlock & Leverage Your U

Your turn! Complete at based on what you understand about your type of super from both the Hero's and Heroine's Journey and IKIGAI experience. Mix it up. There are no rules. Just draw from what you understand and become the *storyteller* rather than the hero or heroine. Be sure to use "ordinary world" language and not Be Your Type of Super specific words like, "my ordeal," or "my call to adventure," or my threshold," etc.!

The external aspect of the U may not be as easy to figure out. You research and go with what you know. You should know about the organization and its mission, how it seeks to serve others. An understanding of the reward will happen during the interview. Note it when it happens so you understand how to tweak your U.

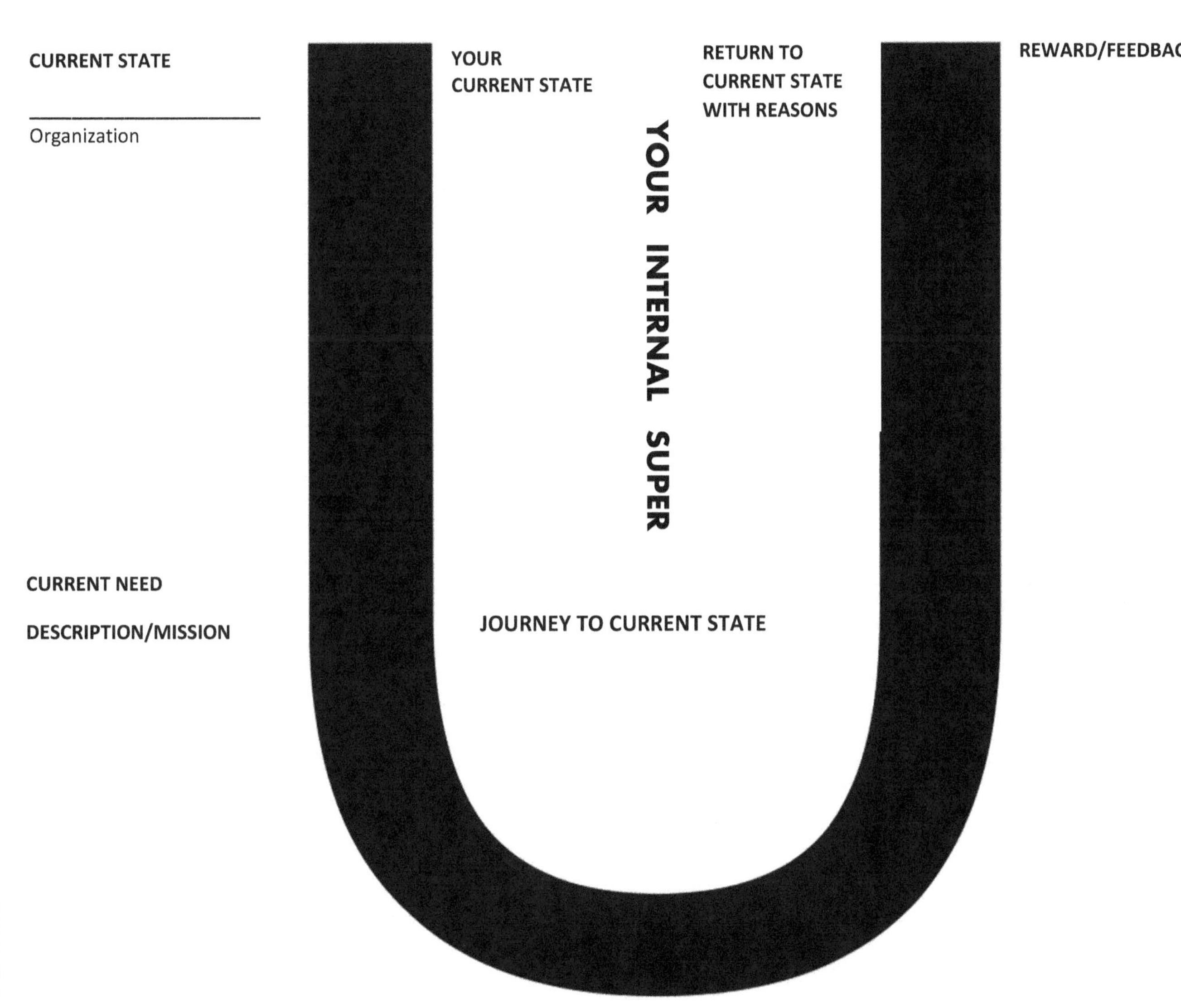

When Did You Learn About Sharing Your Journey?

WAYS TO LEVERAGE BE YOUR TYPE OF SUPER

Super Your Resume

OBJECTIVE	IKIGAI In Ordinary World Language To Make It Easy To Find You
JOB DESCRIPTIONS	• Add ALL Your Rewards Including: Shadowing, Different Roles During Your Hero's Or Heroine's Journey. • Include Your Return, What You Accomplished To Take Back To The Ordinary World. • Structure Your Descriptions To Be Lead Ins For Your U Stories At The Interview • Weave Your Type Of Super Into Every Job Description So That The Reader Can See The Common Thread Coming Through
SKILLS	• List Your Talents And Gifts Here

SUPER Personal Statement

- Let Your Passion Shine Here (Combination Of What You Love Or Are A Stand For And Your Gifts And Talents)
- Tell U Stories Here. Take The Reader On Mini Hero's Or Heroine's Journeys.
- Be Clear About The Return, The Reward You Brought Back And Your Reflection.
- Use Your Top Three Values When You Describe Yourself And What Really Matters.

Super Your Senior Portfolio

- Leverage Your Super Archetypes To Tell Of Your Story Of How You Intentionally Made High School An Adventure To Be With What You Were Learning About Yourself
- Highlight Your Teachers And Educational Community That Were Mentors During Your Journey
- Use Your High School Hero's & Heroine's Journeys To Tell Your Story

Super Meals: Feed Your Super

- Feed You Super So That It Continues To Grow
- Flood Your Feeds With Good Content That Feeds Your Super
- Follow People Who Are Amazing At Your Type Of Super (Easy Mentorship)
- Read Up On Your Type Of Super

Host A Be Your Type Of Super Club

- Have Group Be Your Type Of Super Experiences With Your Peers
- You Need An Adult Sponsor But The Activities Are To Be Peer Facilitated
- Email Info@Denawiggins.Com For More Information

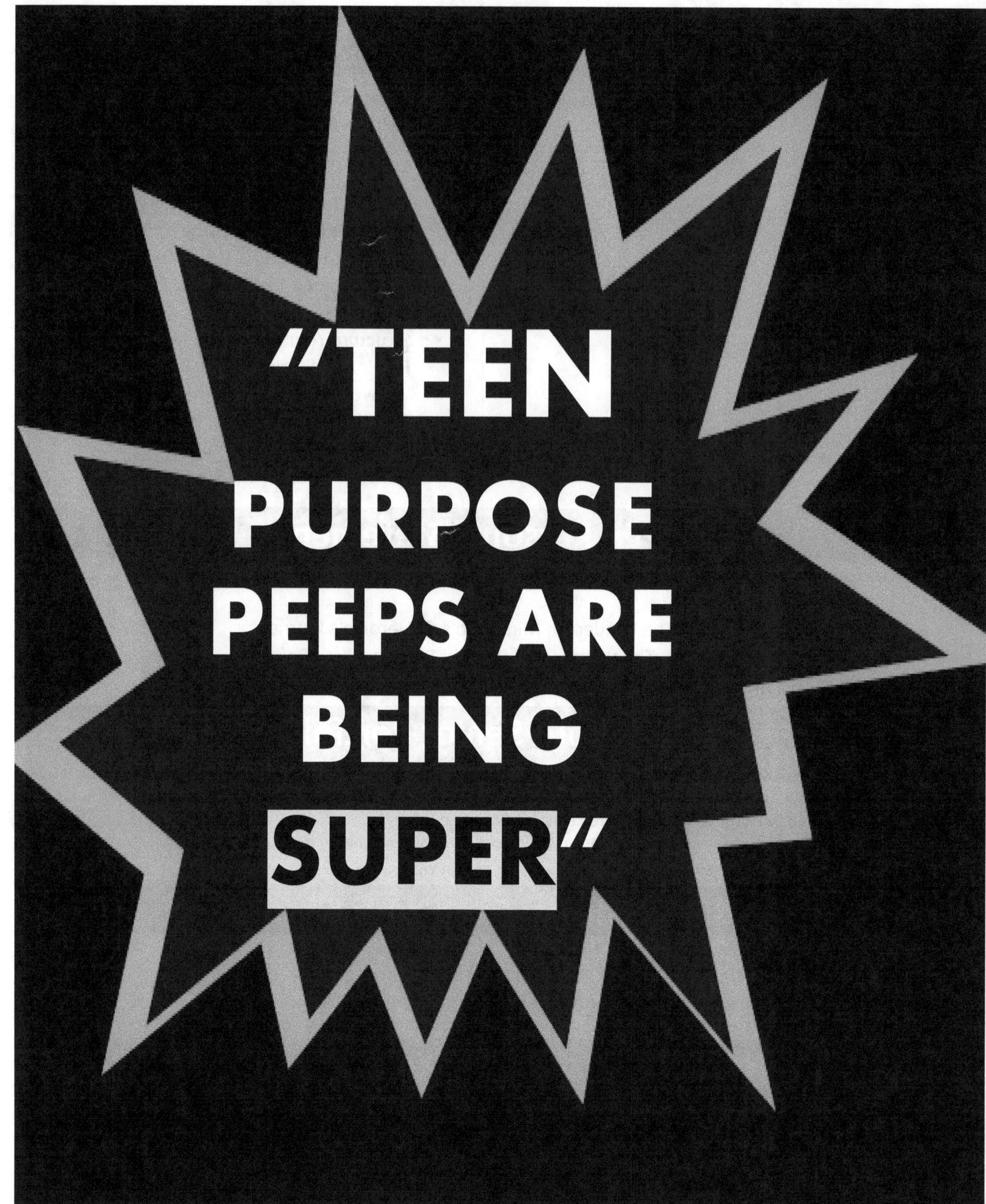
"TEEN
PURPOSE
PEEPS ARE
BEING
SUPER"

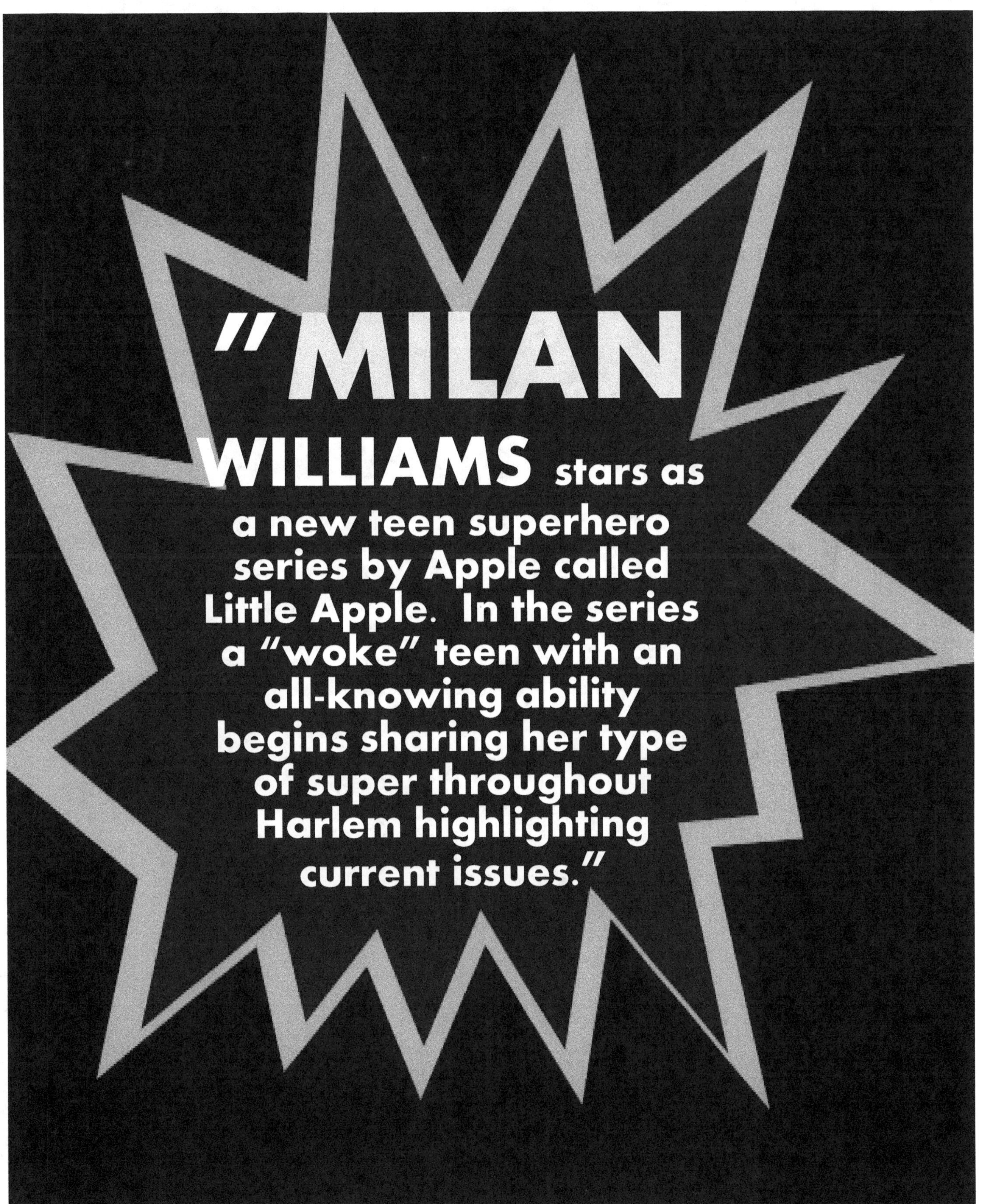
"MILAN
WILLIAMS stars as
a new teen superhero
series by Apple called
Little Apple. In the series
a "woke" teen with an
all-knowing ability
begins sharing her type
of super throughout
Harlem highlighting
current issues."

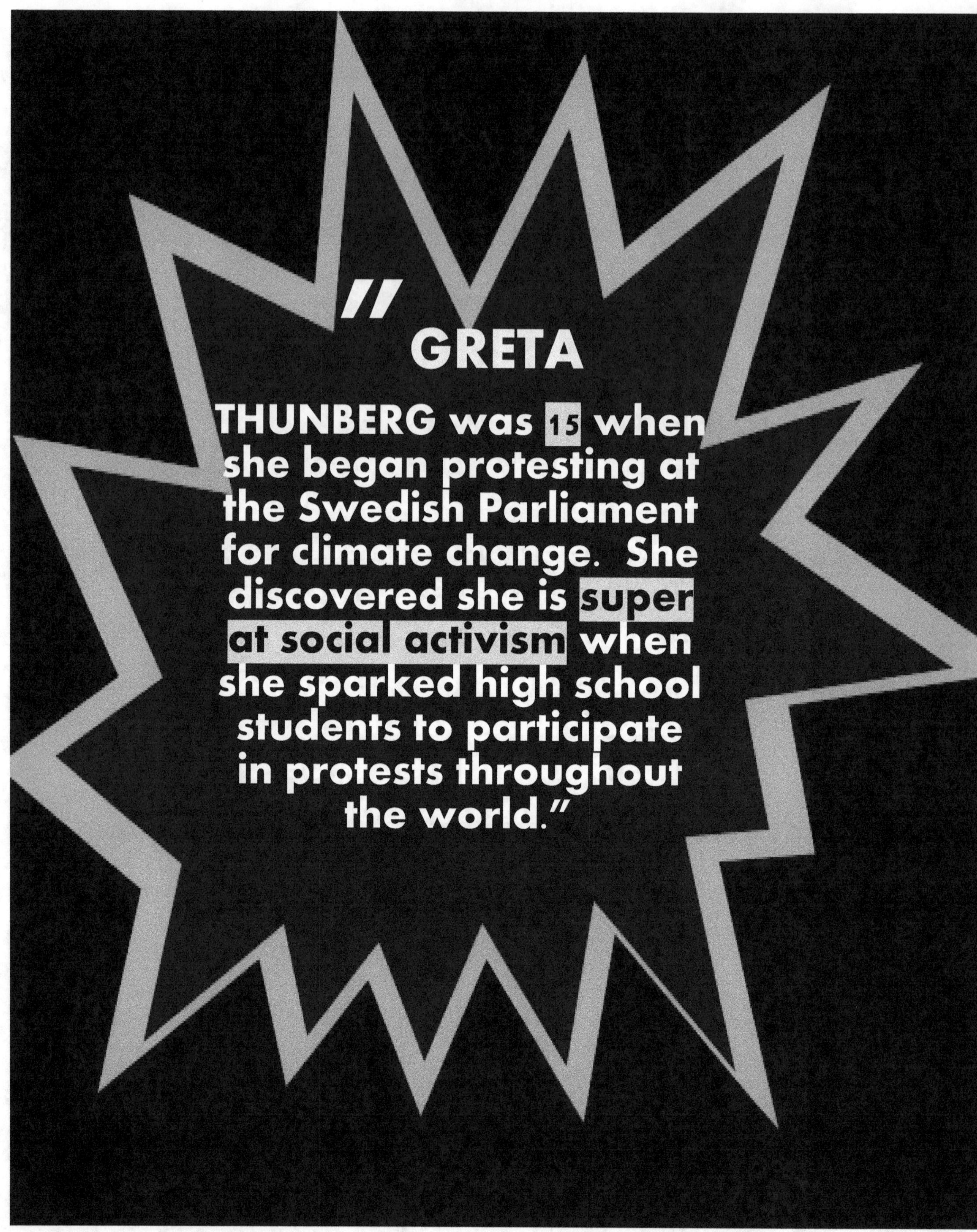
"
GRETA
THUNBERG was 15 when she began protesting at the Swedish Parliament for climate change. She discovered she is super at social activism when she sparked high school students to participate in protests throughout the world."

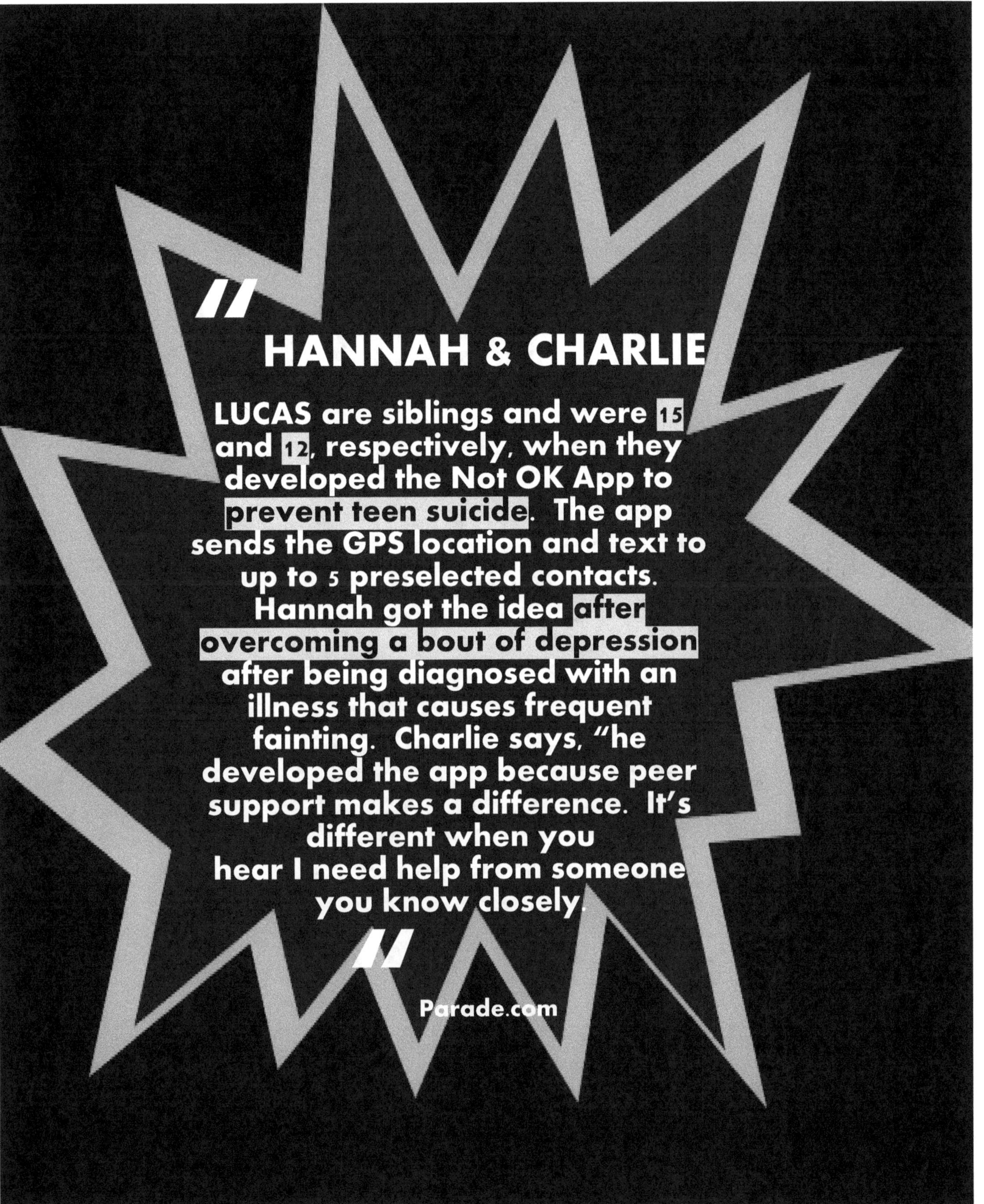
"
HANNAH & CHARLIE
LUCAS are siblings and were 15
and 12, respectively, when they
developed the Not OK App to
prevent teen suicide. The app
sends the GPS location and text to
up to 5 preselected contacts.
Hannah got the idea after
overcoming a bout of depression
after being diagnosed with an
illness that causes frequent
fainting. Charlie says, "he
developed the app because peer
support makes a difference. It's
different when you
hear I need help from someone
you know closely.
"
Parade.com

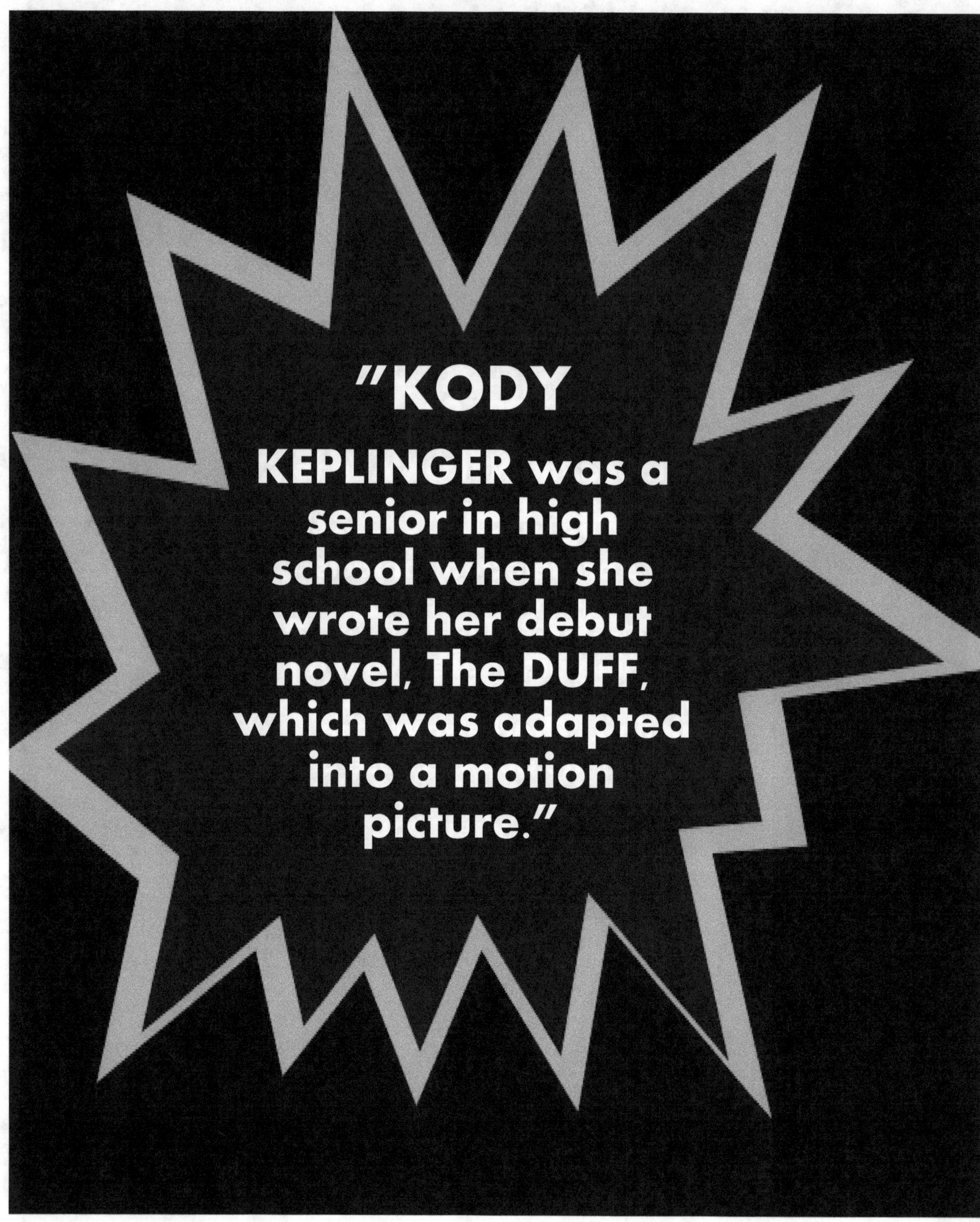
"KODY
KEPLINGER was a
senior in high
school when she
wrote her debut
novel, The DUFF,
which was adapted
into a motion
picture."

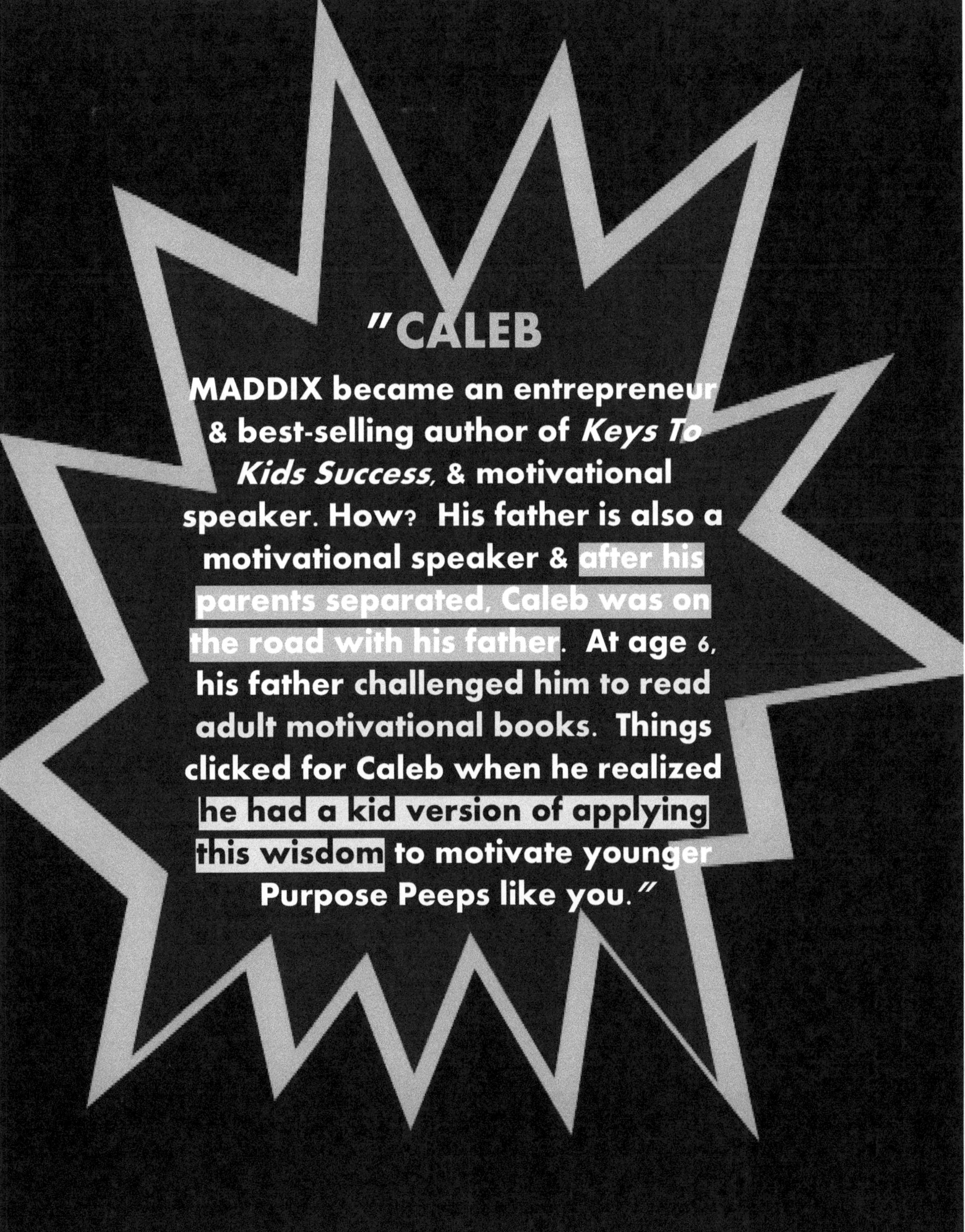
"CALEB
MADDIX became an entrepreneur & best-selling author of *Keys To Kids Success,* & motivational speaker. How? His father is also a motivational speaker & after his parents separated, Caleb was on the road with his father. At age 6, his father challenged him to read adult motivational books. Things clicked for Caleb when he realized he had a kid version of applying this wisdom to motivate younger Purpose Peeps like you."

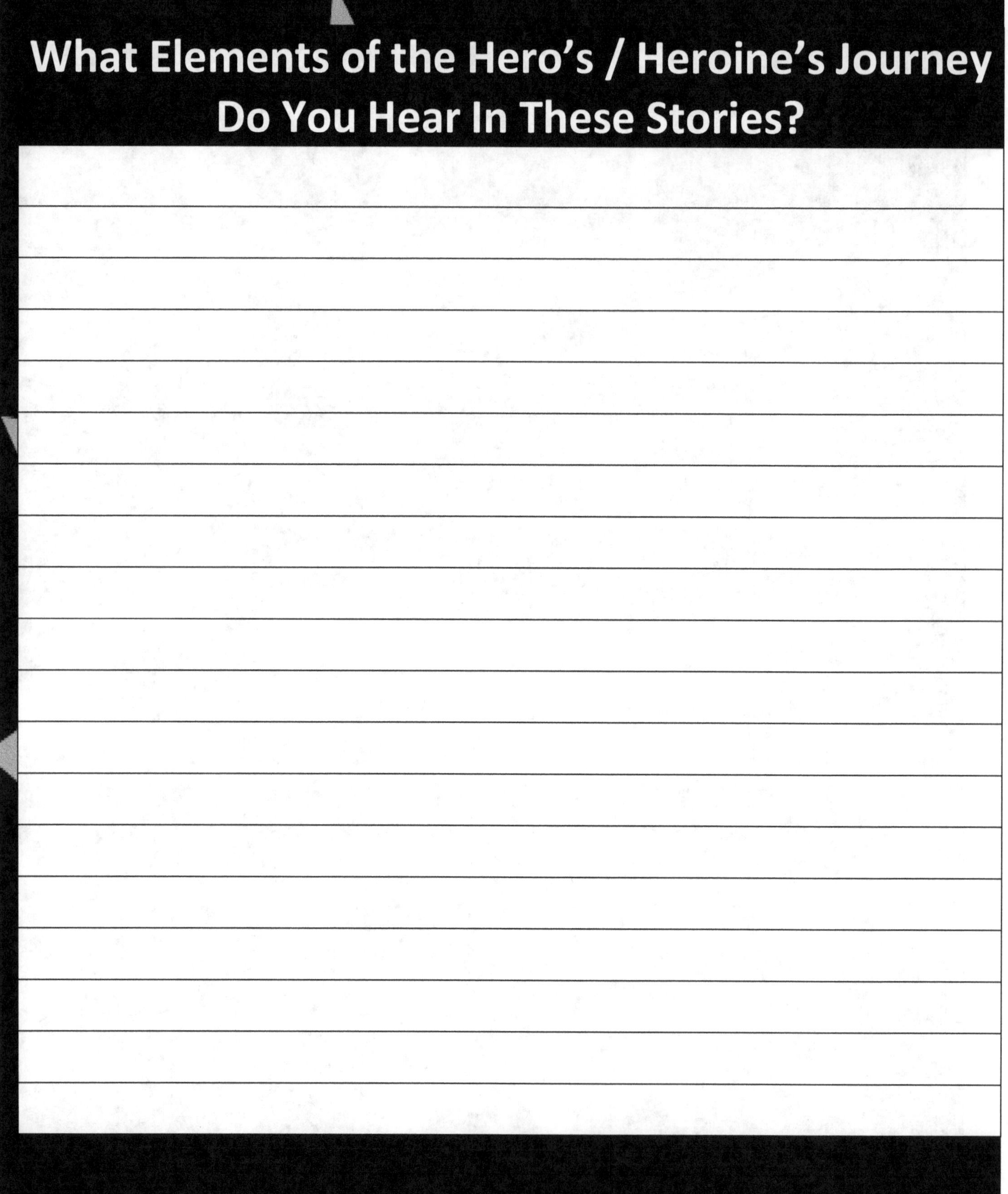
What Elements of the Hero's / Heroine's Journey
Do You Hear In These Stories?

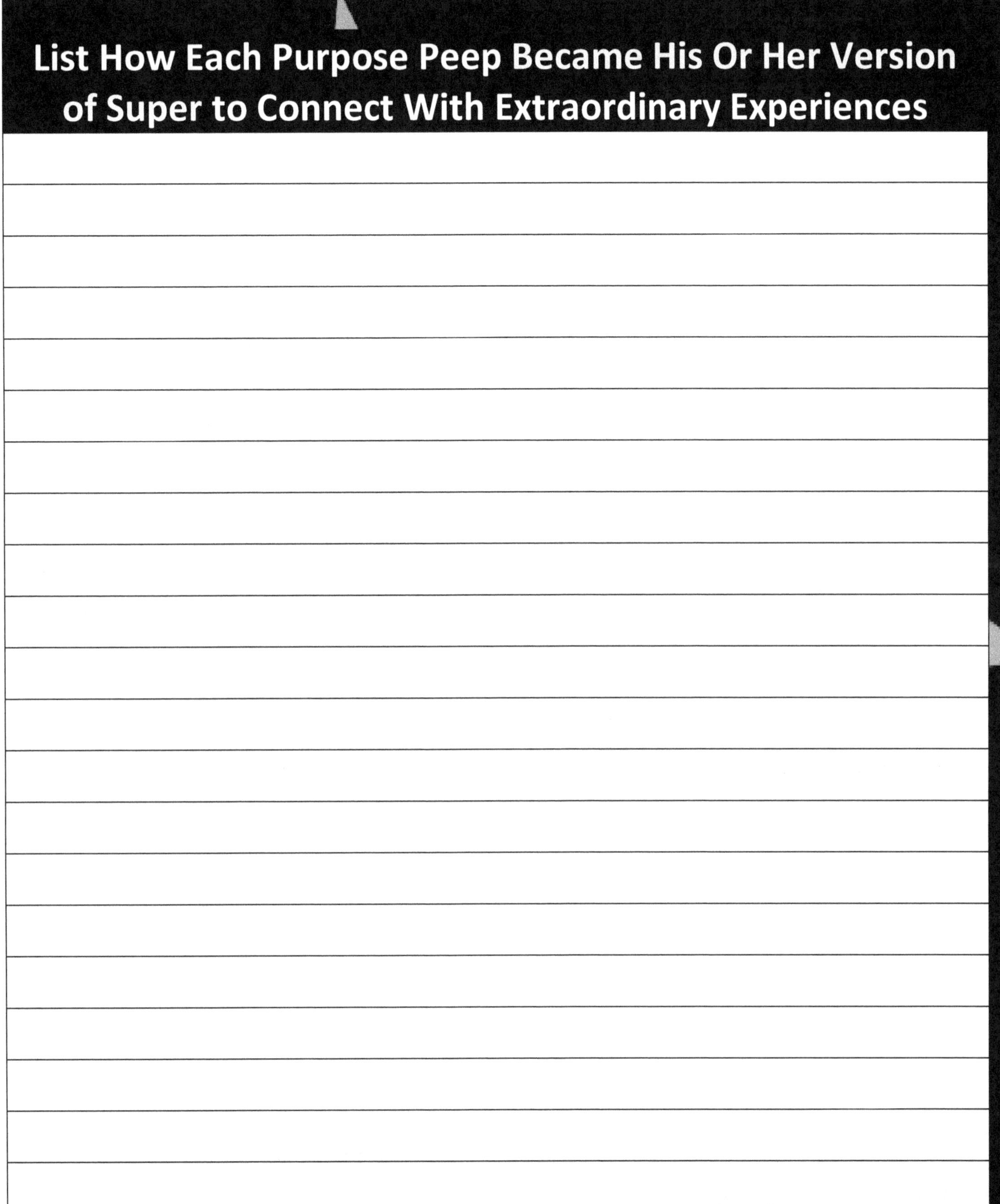
List How Each Purpose Peep Became His Or Her Version of Super to Connect With Extraordinary Experiences

WHAT'S NEXT?

GO BE SUPER!!!!

SHARE YOUR SUPER WITH BE YOUR TYPE OF SUPER GEAR

HAVE ADVENTURES. GET TO KNOW YOUR SUPER

PRACTICE BEING SUPPORTING ROLES IN THE JOURNEY OF ANOTHER HERO'S OR HEROINE'S JOURNEY

PARTNER WITH OTHER TYPES OF SUPERS.

USE THE FOLLOWING BLANK SHEETS AFTER YOUR NEXT CALLS TO ADVENTURE TO REVIEW THE ADVENTURE...

OR WHEN YOU NEED TO REMEMBER THE HERO OR HEROINE IN YOU

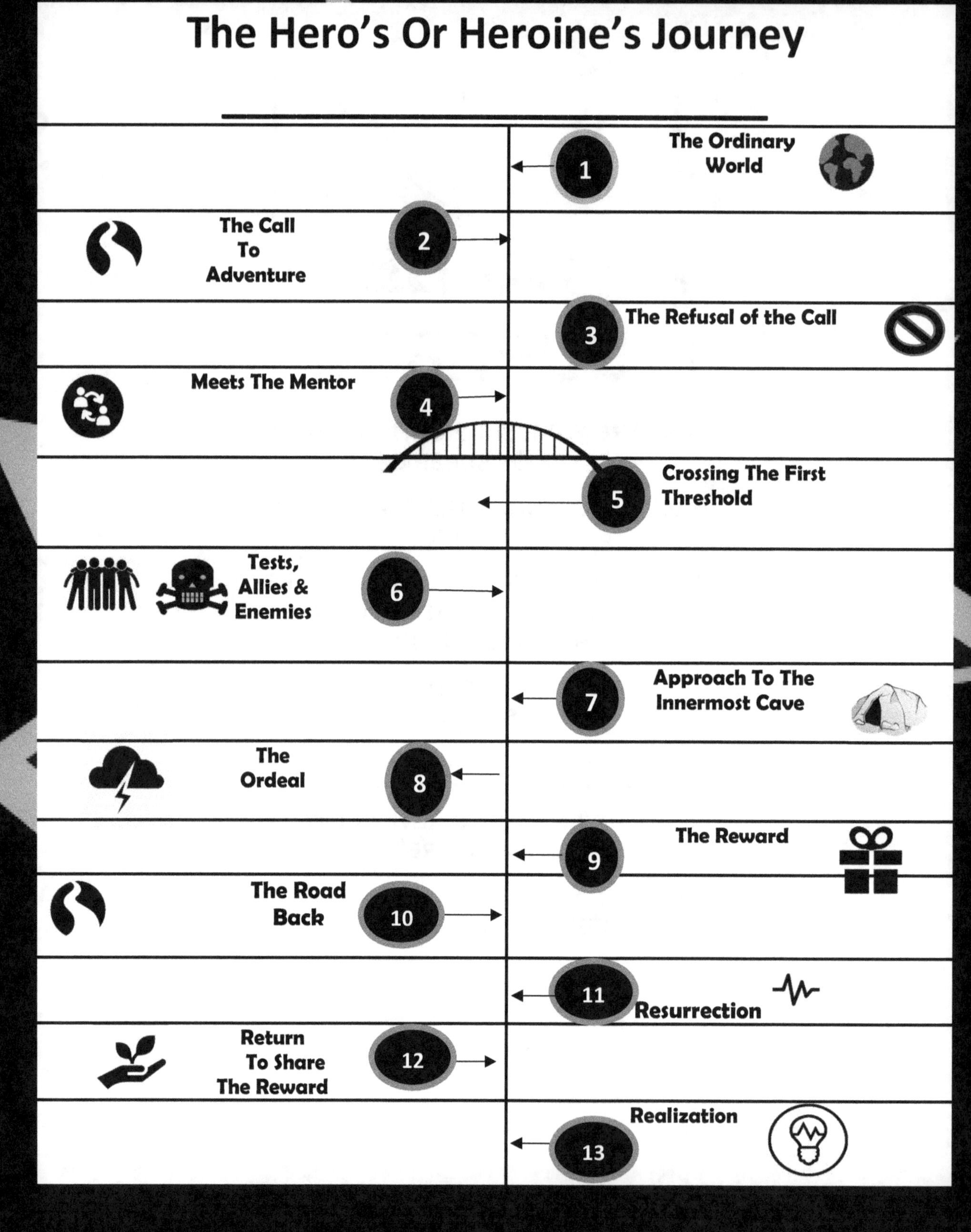
The Hero's Or Heroine's Journey
1
The Ordinary World
2
The Call To Adventure
3
The Refusal of the Call
4
Meets The Mentor
5
Crossing The First Threshold
6
Tests, Allies & Enemies
7
Approach To The Innermost Cave
8
The Ordeal
9
The Reward
10
The Road Back
11
Resurrection
12
Return To Share The Reward
13
Realization

The Hero's / Heroine's Journey Relationship Reflection

Who Are Your Mentors That Believe You Can Do It?

Who Are Your Allies That Share Your Goals & Direction?

Who Are Your Friends, Your Tribe That Are There In Good Times & Bad Times?

The Hero's / Heroine's Journey Impact Reflection

What Moves You Out of Your Ordinary World (Comfort Zone)?

What Are You Really Passionate About?

Who Receives The Gifts You Take Back To The Ordinary World?

The Hero's / Heroine's Journey Growth Reflection

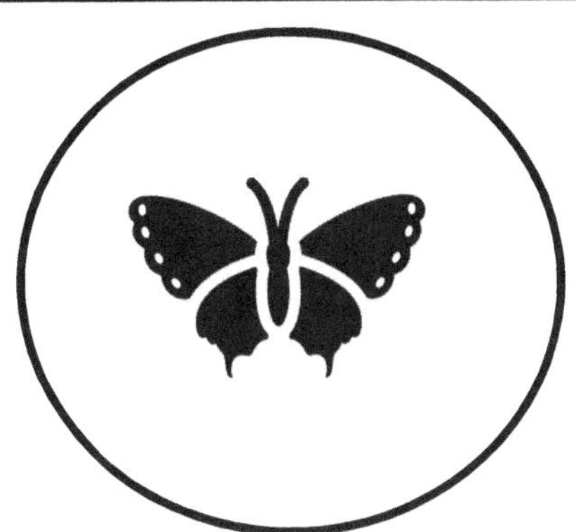

What Changed From The Beginning of Your Journey To Now?

What skills or knowledge are you building?

Who Supports How You Are Growing & Changing?

Super Orbit Questionnaire

Name	Ally, Enemy, Friend, Frenemy, or Mentor	How Do You Feel In Her/His Presence? Expansive, Small, Etc.	After 90 Days	Experience During a Challenge, Shift or Change?	After Another 90 Days	Experience During a Challenge, Shift or Change?

Ally	Shares the same goal or mission with you. When the mission is over, the relationship may be over
Enemy	Shows up either/and against you or what you show up or take a stand for
Friend	Cares for you personally, you have things in common and shows up for you even when he or she may not agree with what you stand for
Frenemy	A friend who strongly disagrees with your direction or what you stand for
Mentor	Believes in you and your general possibility or in a specific area and because of that shares, guides, shares wisdom or tools to help move you along to your goals

Super Tips:

- ✓ Complete from the perspective of you on your hero's or heroine's journey. Sometimes people relate to you differently when you are changing than when you are in the ordinary world.
- ✓ If people reveal they cannot hang during times of challenge, cool, do not expect them to and just chill with them. Everyone needs people they can come back to from adventures and just chill.
- ✓ Sometimes the most impactful change is in how we relate to people and not expecting more from them than they can give.
- ✓ You can complete your Posse Inventory at the beginning or end of each grade.
- ✓ If there is a difference between what you think and what you feel in your body, go with what you feel in your body.

Super Orbit Exercise

Complete this exercise from the perspective of you and what you understand about your super! This is the version of you that is in the center. Your orbiting relationships surround you from most personal to least personal. The enemy is in the outer orbit, furthest from you because the energy and intention of this person(s) is like kryptonite for your emerging super, right now. Things can change and yet the decisions you make NOW impact whether your super flourishes and matures or diminishes and dies out.

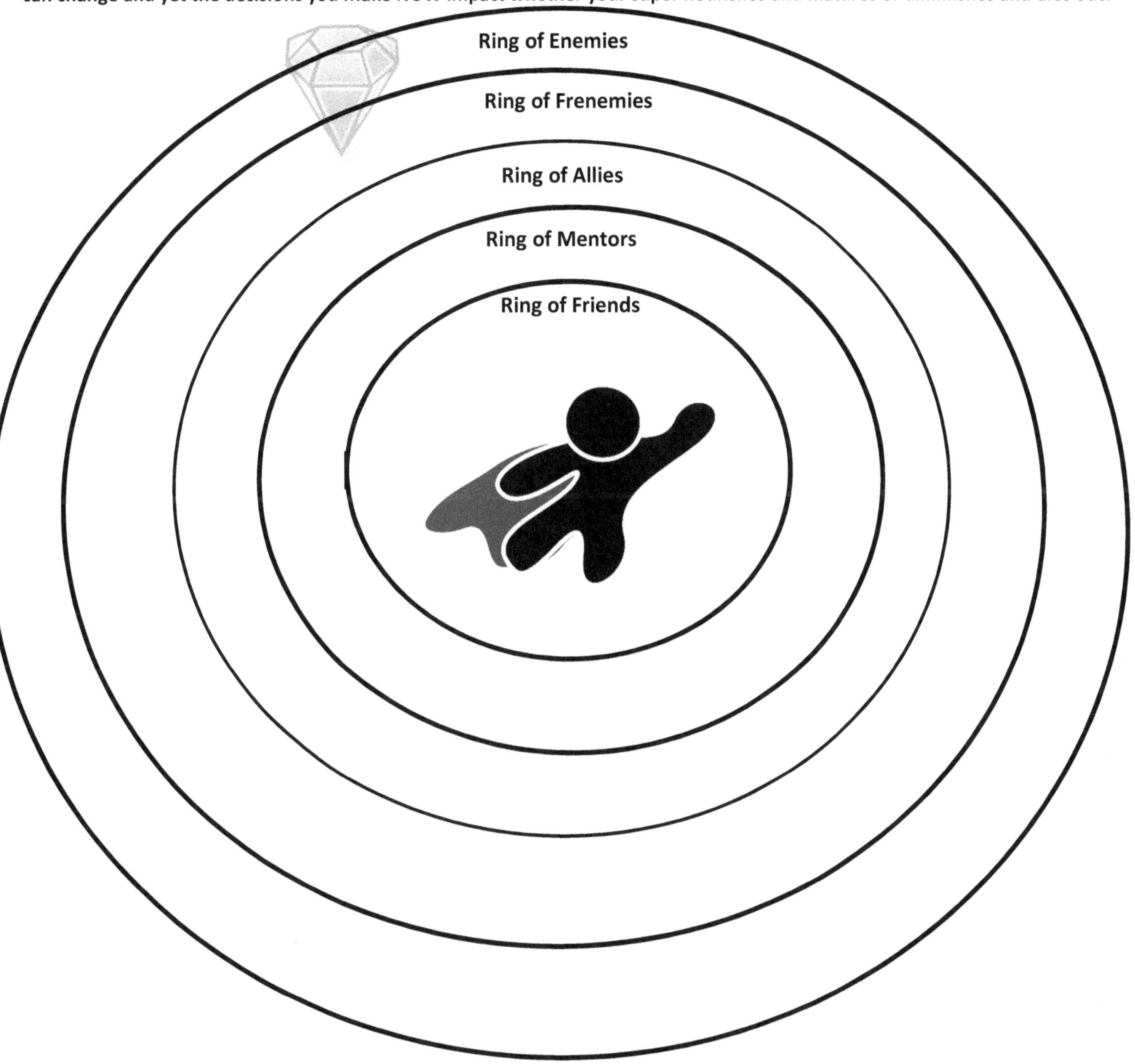

IKIGAI

Complete Using Your Hero's Or Heroine's Journey

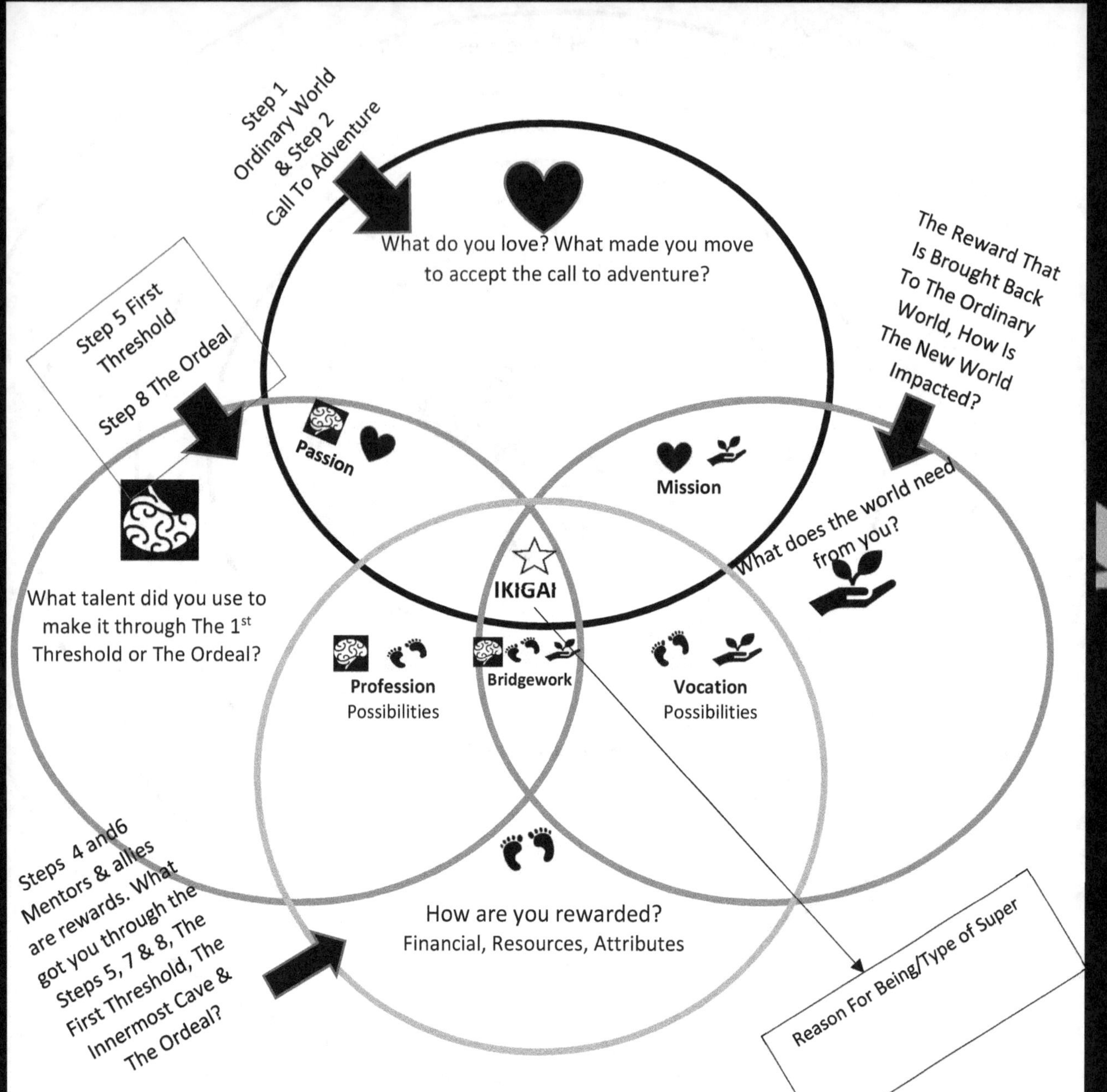

Super Tip: Start with the main circles first (heart, head, feet, hand) then branch out to the transitional areas. Look at the content of your answers within the main circles to create combinations for the transitional areas.

It's		20__

My Top 3 Values Are:		My Type of Super Is
4.		I initially accepted or refused this type of super because:
5.		My super is influenced by these major events:
6.		4.
My Super Orbit Is:		5.
Friends/Allies/Mentors:		6.
Frenemies/Enemies:		

	The things I love or take a stand for are:
	My experiences with these people, places or things are:
	I learned:
	I am really gifted at/talented in the area(s) of:
	My experiences in being with this aspect of my type of super are:
	I learned:
	What the world needs from me is/are:
	My experiences with being with my impact are:
	I learned:
	My rewards for rocking out my type of super are:
	My experiences with being rewarded are:
	I learned:
What I liked about this experience:	
What I disliked about this experience:	
How I would choose differently & why:	

IKIGAI Your Goals

Reminder: IKIGAI Is Not Perfection, It Is Where Your Inner Super & Ordinary World Needs Meet To Have Extraordinary Experiences. Your Transitional Areas Move You Toward IKIGAI. Use Them!

1. Review Your IKIGAI

Complete Using Your Hero's Or Heroine's Journey

2. Circle The Main Area(s) Where You Have A Lot of Understanding

Look at your current goals and see where they fit in the IGIKAI areas. Set a goal to remain strong in this area. What are your reps that strengthen this area?

3. Circle The Main Area(s) Where You Have Less Clarity

Set a goal to be more tuned in to new info in this area. When your next call to adventure happens, notice how it is building your awareness in one or more of these areas.

Review Your Transition Areas

Passion Profession

Vocation Bridgework

As you plan for the future, review where your goals fall in IKIGAI and adjust accordingly. The goal is not perfection but for your inner super to connect with the needs of the ordinary world in a way that rewards you providing grounding for you.

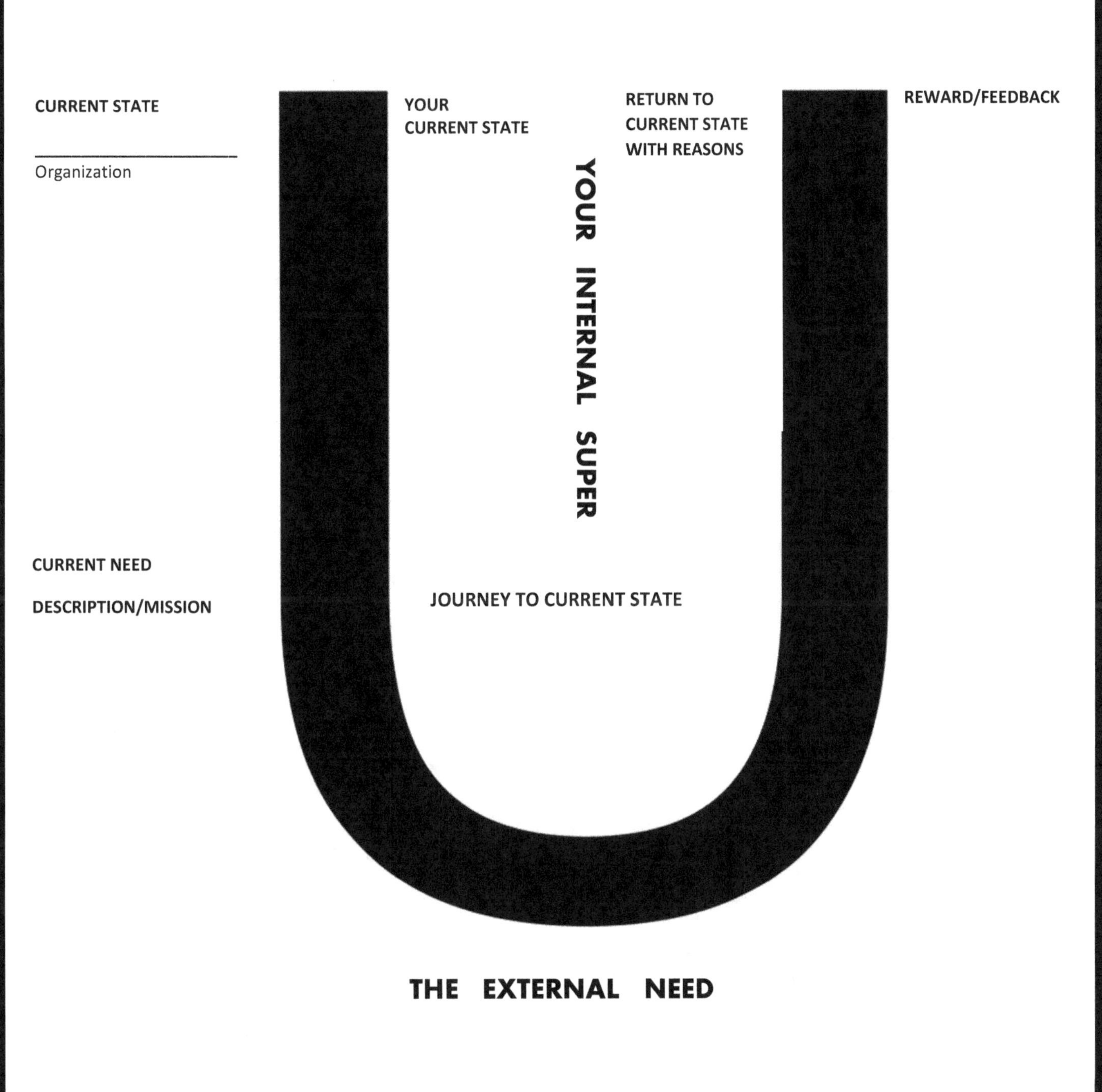
CURRENT STATE
Organization
YOUR
CURRENT STATE
RETURN TO
CURRENT STATE
WITH REASONS
REWARD/FEEDBACK
YOUR INTERNAL SUPER
CURRENT NEED
DESCRIPTION/MISSION
JOURNEY TO CURRENT STATE
THE EXTERNAL NEED

Visit bit.ly/Purpose Place For New Workbooks, Experiences & Gear & Be Your Type of Super Clubs & Chapters (Coming Soon)

Email questions to info@denawiggins.com

Hashtag #BeYourTypeOfSuper #MyTypeOfSuper #MySuperpowerIs to share your super with others

Get Your Be Your Type of Super Gear at bit.ly/PurposePlace

www.ingramcontent.com/pod-product-compliance
Lightning Source LLC
LaVergne TN
LVHW061248100826
845148LV00008B/1062